She Wore Her Scars

Like Wings

A MEMOIR OF PAIN, POWER AND REBIRTH

By

Lisa Ortiz

CONTENTS

PROLOGUE

As I sit here in this four-walled cell, I wonder: what is my motive for writing my story? I've spent so much time wanting to tell someone, but it's all been bottled up inside. I've never been the type of person to have friends. I'm always suspicious of everyone because I've been told nothing in life is free. Every time I've let someone in, they've stabbed me in the back. Today, I am 34 years old. I have five beautiful children who are out there in society, left to navigate life without me because of my own faults and choices. Now that I'm older, I realize that just because life wasn't handed to me on a silver platter, that didn't mean I had to break the law. But I did. And because of that, I have spent almost all my years behind these walls. But the saddest truth of all? This place feels like home. Other than my five kids, this is the only family I've ever known. People think they know me. They swear they can read my emotions and understand my feelings. But they don't. No one truly knows me. No one understands what I've endured. But now, it's time to tell the world.

My name is Lisa Marie Acker Ortiz Fundora, and this is my story.

Pain

A simple touch, a simple word, a simple saying—pain.

A simple slap, a simple hit, a simple bruise, a simple cut—pain.

No love, no remorse, no tears, no recourse—pain.

Dedicated to me, Lisa Acker

CHAPTER 1
THE BEGINNING

I was born in Brooklyn, New York, on May 5, 1976. My brother Luis followed right behind me, born on April 27, 1977. We were less than a year apart—what some folks call "Irish twins." Our birthdays were so close that it almost felt like we shared a heartbeat. But even as kids, we would come to learn that closeness in birth doesn't always mean closeness in life.

From what I was told, my mother was a beautiful, chocolate-skinned Black woman. People said she had long, glossy black hair that flowed down her back like a silk curtain. Her smile? Radiant. The kind that could light up a block. They said she had a way of walking into a room and making everyone pause—not just because of her looks, but because of her presence. She was about my height and build, and from all accounts, she was striking. Elegant, even. The kind of woman people remembered.

But I don't remember her. Not really. I never saw her—not in the way a child is supposed to see their mother holding them, guiding them, rocking them to sleep. My memories of her are secondhand, passed down like rumors, like fading photographs in the minds of others. I used to sit quietly as family or neighbors shared glimpses of her—little snapshots of who she was before the addiction took hold. I would listen and try to stitch together a mother from fragments.

But the truth is, my mother was a junkie. That's not easy to say. Not because it's a secret but because it's a wound. She loved drugs more than she loved her children. And that's a sentence I've had to wrestle with most of my life. Not because I blame her—not entirely—but because I wanted her to fight harder for us. For me. For Luis. I wanted her to choose us. But addiction is a thief. It robs people of their choices, their clarity, and their capacity to love in ways that matter.

Growing up without her was like walking through life with an invisible limp. You get used to the pain, but the imbalance is always there. There were birthdays where I waited, hoping she'd appear. Hoped she'd remember.

She never did. There were school plays, scraped knees, nightmares, and milestones—and she wasn't there for any of them. Instead, I had to learn what love looked like from scraps: a kind neighbor who gave us extra bread, a teacher who lingered a little longer after class, a foster parent who tucked us in with the kind of gentleness we didn't know we needed.

There was always a part of me that wondered what might've been different if she had just gotten clean. If she had gotten help. If someone had reached her before the drugs did. And there were nights—quiet, restless nights—when I hated her for it. Hated that her absence shaped so much of my story. Hated that I had to carry the weight of her decisions before I was even old enough to spell my name.

But time does something strange. As I got older, that hate softened. Not into love, exactly, but into understanding. I came to realize that people don't become addicted because they want to destroy their families. They do it because something inside them is already breaking. I don't know what broke her. I may never know. Maybe it was trauma, pain, loneliness—demons she couldn't outrun. But whatever it was, it stole her from us long before the streets did.

And still, some part of me hopes she had moments of clarity— moments where she thought about me and Luis. Maybe she whispered our names when no one was around. Maybe she prayed in her own way. Maybe she even wished she had done it differently. I like to believe that. I have to believe that. Because it helps me carry the pain with a little more grace.

She gave me life, even if she couldn't give me love. And somehow, I've taken that life and built something out of it. Something strong. Something grounded. Something she might've been proud of if she'd had the chance to know me.

Early Life

My mother left me and my baby brother in an abandoned apartment building in the middle of the projects in Brooklyn. Nobody knows how long we stayed in that crib, but we did—dirty and hungry. Just two little boys, alone in a space that wasn't meant to hold life, only echoes. The kind of place people pass by without looking twice. The kind of silence that didn't come with peace but with neglect. The walls around us were crumbling, the floor cold, the air thick with a kind of emptiness you could feel in your bones. We must have cried, or maybe we stopped crying after a while. Maybe our small bodies learned early that crying didn't bring help, didn't bring food, didn't bring her back.

It's hard to imagine what goes through a mother's mind when she leaves her babies behind. Maybe she told herself she'd be right back. Maybe she believed someone else would find us. Maybe she couldn't bear to look us in the eyes while walking away. Whatever the reason, she left. And we stayed. Me and my brother, barely more than babies, trying to survive without knowing what survival even meant. Time doesn't move the same when you're abandoned. Minutes stretch into something darker. Hunger isn't just a feeling in your stomach—it becomes part of your skin, your breath, your thoughts. We were too young to name what we felt, but our bodies knew something was wrong. Deeply wrong.

This is what I know about my father: absolutely nothing. Not his name. Not his face. Not his story. Nothing. The only thing I know is that he was not a Black man. That alone made me different, even in ways I couldn't understand at the time. I carried that difference in my skin, in my reflection, in the way people sometimes looked at me and tried to guess the rest. But heritage doesn't mean much when it comes to silence. When there's no history to hold onto—only a question mark.

To be honest, he must've loved my mother—at least for a moment—because he's my brother's father as well. And that tells me something. It tells me they were together long enough for two lives to begin. Two lives to be born. Maybe he believed in her. Maybe he tried. Or maybe he was as lost as she was. But somewhere in the mix of chaos and craving, addiction and absence, two children came into the world. And then, one by one, the adults disappeared.

That's the truth I carry. Not dramatic, not glamorous—just raw. Just real. And even though I have no memories of him, no photographs, no old letters or stories passed down, I sometimes wonder if he ever thought of us. If he ever looked back. If he ever walked past a playground, saw two kids playing, and felt a hollow ache in his chest, he couldn't explain. Maybe he did. Maybe he didn't. But I'm here. And so is my brother. And somehow, we made it out of that crib. Dirty, hungry, forgotten—but alive.

Maybe my dad was some type of trick or a drug dealer, or maybe he was a rich man—or just maybe he was a junkie too. Truth is, I've played every version of him in my mind, trying to make sense of the ghost. Sometimes, I imagined him as some smooth-talking hustler who slid in and out of my mother's life like smoke. Other times, I pictured a man in a suit, someone with money, power, and access—someone who kept our existence a secret because we didn't fit the story he wanted to live. And then there were the darker days when I imagined him strung out somewhere, lost in the same cycle that swallowed her whole. No strength to save himself, let alone save two sons he never claimed.

But I've always said that he must have loved my mother because she had both of us. That fact alone meant something to me growing up. Two children by the same man in a life full of chaos? That didn't happen by accident. There had to have been a season where love, or at least something close to it, existed between them. I held onto that idea more than I realized, like a thread connecting me to something warmer, something more human. Maybe it was a lie, or maybe it was the only truth I had.

If that was the case—if he had love for her—he would have taken care of us. That's the part that stings. Because love isn't just a feeling; it's a responsibility. It's what you do when no one is watching. And if he really loved her, if he really cared, then why did he let us rot in that crib? Why didn't he come looking for us? I try not to sit in that question too long because it leads nowhere good. But it lingers. It always lingers.

And maybe—just maybe—if he had stepped up, if he had chosen us, if he had been man enough to carry what he helped create, maybe our life would be so much different. Maybe we would've grown up with stability, with protection, with the kind of love that builds instead of breaks. Maybe we wouldn't have had to learn how to survive before we even knew how to read. Maybe we would've known what it felt like to be chosen fully, completely, and without condition.

But all I have is maybe. A father-shaped silence. A legacy of what-ifs.

And yet, I'm still here. Still standing. Still rising.

Orphanage Days

So here we were, in a crib for God knows how long after our mother left us. She never came back. The days must've bled into each other—shadows on the wall, silence that felt like thunder. There was no voice to soothe us, no arms to hold us, no one to say, "It's okay." Just two small kids in a forgotten corner of the world, left behind like trash in an empty building. Sometimes, I wonder how we made it. Who found us. What we looked like when they did. Were we crying? Sleeping? Just staring off into that space where innocence goes to hide?

I remember going to the orphanage and holding a Raggedy Ann doll everywhere I went. It wasn't new. It wasn't even clean. But to me, it was everything. That doll was the only constant in a life full of strangers and echoes. Something about the way it sat in my arms made me feel like maybe I wasn't alone. Maybe someone or something was still with me. It became my shield, my friend, my comfort in a world I didn't understand. I was three; my brother was two. We were babies trying to carry the weight of abandonment like grown men. The system didn't slow down for our pain. It just processed us.

No emotion can describe the way I felt. Not fear. Not sadness. Not even anger. It was something deeper. Something wordless. Like a hollow inside my chest that nothing could fill. I didn't cry all the time. I think I learned early that tears didn't change anything. But I remember feeling cold—not from the weather, but from the ache of being forgotten. That's a different kind of cold. The kind that gets inside your bones and stays there.

I held onto Luis tightly—tighter than I held that doll. He was the only piece of home I had left. The only person in the whole world who knew exactly what I was going through because he was going through it, too. I don't remember talking much. We didn't need words. We had each other. We held hands in silence. We leaned into each other in those unfamiliar beds, in those cold waiting rooms, in the dark places where children aren't supposed to be. I became his protector, even though I was still a child myself. Somehow, I knew I had to be strong for him. If I let go, we might both fall.

And so I didn't.

We were shown to families like we were prize dogs: "Oh, they're so cute!" That's what they'd say—smiling, pointing, tilting their heads like they were looking through a storefront window. I remember the way the adults would crouch down and talk to us in soft voices like they were picking out a pet or trying to guess how much work we'd be doing. Nobody asked us anything. Nobody wondered what we'd been through. They just wanted to see if we'd fit into their picture.

But they could only take one of us for some reason. Over and over, we heard it: "We'd love to take one of them, but not both." Like we were some kind of bundle deal that people weren't willing to commit to. As if separating us wouldn't tear us apart. I didn't understand why back then, but I felt it. Every time someone smiled at Luis and not me, or at me and not him, it felt like being split down the middle. They kept Luis and me as a package deal for a while, probably because we were so young and so close in age. Maybe someone in the system knew that separating us too early would do damage. Maybe they cared. Maybe not. But we stayed together, and I held onto that with everything I had.

Finally, a Spanish lady named Anna Ortiz came along with her husband, José Ortiz. They looked at our pretty skin and beautiful brown eyes and fell in love with us—or so I thought. I remember the way Anna smiled at us. Her eyes lit up like we were exactly what she'd been searching for. José was quieter, but he nodded along, hand resting on her back like a seal of approval. It felt hopeful. Like maybe this was it. Maybe we had been chosen. Maybe, finally, we were wanted.

I wanted to believe it. I needed to believe it. After everything we'd been through—the hunger, the cold, the silence, the crib, the doll, the confusion—this felt like the beginning of something better. A home. A family. Love.

Or so I thought.

New Home

We started living with them about one month after we met them. The papers were signed, the system did its routine checkbox, and just like that, we had a new last name and a new address. We moved into a house in Vernon, New Jersey, a quiet place with winding streets and trees that changed with the seasons. It was nothing like Brooklyn. No sirens. No shouting neighbors. No cold cement stairwells. Just silence, grass, and a front porch that felt almost too peaceful to be real.

Anna had four kids of her own: Mikey, Evelyn, Virginia, and Juan. They were all older than us, but not by much, and they all seemed pretty nice—at least in the beginning. There was a polite kind of curiosity in the air, like we were guests they weren't sure would be staying. But they didn't push us away. They smiled, shared their toys, and tried to include us. It was the first time I had ever lived with so many people under one roof, and there was something oddly comforting about the noise of it—doors opening, feet running, someone always talking or laughing in another room.

They made us this big bedroom in the basement with circus wallpaper on the walls. It was bright and a little strange—red and yellow clowns dancing in loops, elephants balancing on balls, trapeze artists frozen in mid-air. Two twin beds sat side by side, neatly made with matching sheets. And next to the beds was a big box full of toys. All kinds. Trucks, blocks, dolls, puzzles—things we'd never had before. It felt like a dream. Like we'd stepped into someone else's life. Someone lucky.

Luis and I would be in our own little world, always playing with each other. No matter how big the house was, no matter how many kids were in it, we stuck close. We had made it through abandonment, through the orphanage, through the uncertainty, and we weren't about to let go now. We'd build forts from blankets, race toy cars across the tile floor, and make up stories that only we understood. The basement became our kingdom, and in it, we were safe, at least for a while.

We'd go outside in the snow; it was one of the first times I remember feeling joy that wasn't tangled with fear. Luis and I would chase each other through the white powder, bundled in too-big coats and hand-me-down boots. Our noses red, our fingers stiff, but we didn't care.

Snow was magic. It blanketed everything, even the past. We laughed freely, not thinking about where we came from—only about where we were.

Anna would comb and twist my hair every morning while she made me beautiful dresses to wear. She had a gentle way of working through my curls, humming softly as her fingers moved. She'd hold my chin up and say, "Look at you, so pretty," before smoothing down the fabric of my dress. And I believed her. I felt pretty. I felt seen. Those mornings were warm in a way I didn't yet know how to question.

Everything seemed like it was going to be okay. For the first time in my short life, I let myself believe that maybe, just maybe, we were home.

Change

Years went by; Luis was five, and I was six—old enough to go to school. Old enough to start carrying responsibilities that most kids our age didn't even know existed. I'd get up in the morning before anyone called my name and play momma. Not because someone asked me to, but because it felt natural. Because in my little heart, I already knew he was mine to look after. We had come into the world together, survived the worst together, and I wasn't going to let anything separate us—not hunger, not strangers, not even time.

I'd put Luis in his clothes, gently guiding his small arms through the sleeves, straightening out his collar like I'd seen grown-ups do. Sometimes, his little fingers fumbled with the buttons, and I'd help without saying a word—just smiling because I wanted him to feel cared for. I wanted him to feel normal, even if nothing about our lives was. Then I'd walk him to the table and make sure he ate his peanut butter sandwich—our staple, our routine, our little comfort.

And every morning, I'd give him half of mine, too. Not because I wasn't hungry. I was always hungry. But I loved him that much. It wasn't even a question in my mind. If there was food to be shared, he got more. If there was warmth, I wanted him to have it. Looking back, I realize I was just a child myself, but in those moments, I felt like something more—like a protector, like his anchor. I didn't have much to give, but what I had, he got. That's what love looked like for me. That's how it lived in my six-year-old body.

Those mornings were quiet acts of devotion. Nobody clapped for them. Nobody even noticed. But they mattered. They built something between us that nothing could touch. A kind of bond forged not just in shared blood but in shared survival.

Struggles

Luis had many health problems; he stayed in and out of the hospital often. I didn't understand all the medical words the doctors used or why his little body seemed to struggle more than most, but I understood this: he was fragile, and he was mine to protect. So I had to make sure he was safe from everyone and everything. I watched over him like a shadow, always close, always alert. If he coughed too hard, I'd worry. If he looked tired, I'd sit beside him a little longer. I became his silent guardian, not because anyone told me to, but because love made me that way.

The world didn't slow down for Luis. It didn't wrap him in care the way he deserved. And the one place that was supposed to feel safe—our home—often felt like a battleground. Anna used to scream at us all the time, her voice sharp like glass, cutting through the air and settling into our bones. There was no warning, no buildup. Just sudden, explosive anger. One moment, she'd be silent, and the next, we were targets for whatever emotion she didn't know how to name.

She'd pull our hair so hard our necks would jerk back like she was trying to yank the pain out of us. But it wasn't about discipline; it was rage. Raw and misplaced. And when her hands weren't enough, she'd reach for whatever was close: an extension cord, a shoe, a belt, her fist. Anything she could get her hands on became a weapon. We learned to flinch at footsteps, to brace ourselves at the sound of her breathing changing.

I tried to shield Luis from it all. Sometimes, I'd stand in front of him. Sometimes, I'd take the blame for things we didn't even do. I thought if I could just be good enough, quiet enough, quick enough, maybe she'd stop. But the truth was, her anger had nothing to do with us. We were just the closest thing she could control. And when someone doesn't know how to heal, they hurt. Over and over.

Still, I stayed close to Luis. Held him after the yelling stopped. Whispered stories to distract him from the bruises. Let him fall asleep curled against me when the nights were too heavy. Because if I couldn't protect him from the pain, I could at least be the one to help him through it.

For some reason, Anna hated me more than Luis; I'm not sure why. I could feel it in the way she looked at me, like my presence annoyed her, like I was a mistake she couldn't return. It wasn't just the yelling or the hitting—it was the coldness, the way her eyes would pass over me like I wasn't even there. I never asked her why she hated me so much or what I did wrong. Maybe I was too scared to hear the answer. Maybe I already believed whatever it was must've been my fault.

All I wanted was for her to love me again like she did when we first arrived. I remember those early days—her hands gently parting my hair, her voice soft as she tied the ribbons on my dresses. She used to smile at me. She used to say I was pretty. And I believed her because every child wants to believe the woman who feeds them and clothes them also loves them. I clung to that early version of her like a faded photograph, hoping that maybe, if I was good enough, quiet enough, helpful enough, she'd return to that softness. That maybe her heart would thaw, and she'd see me again.

But that moment never came.

And every day, I went on pretending not to notice the difference in how she treated us, pretending I didn't ache for something as simple and sacred as a mother's love. I didn't want toys or praise or gifts. I just wanted to feel like I mattered to her.

Even now, part of me still wonders what changed.

Reflection

I used to lie down in my bed while Luis played with cast-off toys from Anna's kids—old plastic soldiers missing limbs, stuffed animals with worn-out fur and stitched-up seams, dolls that had lost their sparkle but still carried stories. He'd line them up, talking to them like they were alive, creating little worlds with whatever scraps he had. Sometimes, he'd try to get me to play, nudging a toy toward my hand, smiling that big, crooked grin of his. But I couldn't always pretend. Not every day. Not when my mind was someplace else.

As I lay there, staring up at the circus wallpaper that had started to peel from the corners, I would drift into thoughts I didn't know how to hold. I'd wonder where my mama was or who she loved now. Did she think about us? Did she remember the shape of our faces? Did she even know we were still alive? Those questions circled my head like whispers I couldn't shake. They came with no answers—only that heavy, hollow feeling of being unwanted.

I had no memories of her, not really. Just shadows. Feelings. An ache that didn't have a picture to go with it. Except for one hazy image I held onto: an older Black lady with salt-and-pepper Afro hair and moles on her cheeks—pretty moles, like mine. That must've been my grandmother. I don't know how I knew, but something in me believed it. There was a softness in her face, a tired kindness that felt familiar, even in a memory I wasn't sure was mine. Maybe I dreamed of her. Maybe she held me once, just long enough to leave an imprint on my spirit. I used to close my eyes and try to remember more: her voice, her scent, the way her hands might've felt on my back. But the details never came. Only that faint vision and the strange comfort it brought.

I'd touch my own cheek sometimes, tracing the little moles I had, pretending they connected me to someone—anyone—who had loved me once. I'd tell myself maybe she had moles, too. Maybe she told my mama stories. Maybe she sang lullabies. No one ever sang to me. In the quiet of that basement bedroom, while Luis pushed toy cars across the floor, I created my own history. A softer one. A safer one. One where I came from, women who loved deeply, who held babies close, who whispered strength into their children before the world got hold of them.

But when the daydreams faded, I was still lying there. Still wondering. Still aching. The truth was, I didn't know where my mama was. I didn't know who she had become. And the silence she left behind felt louder with every year that passed.

One day, while snooping around under the bed, I found a yellow poster with my picture on it saying, "Do you want me?" It was old, curled at the edges, the paper soft like it had been touched too many times or maybe forgotten for too long. My heart jumped when I saw it. I blinked, almost not believing what I was looking at. It was me—small, wide-eyed, uncertain. And in my arms was that beautiful Raggedy Ann doll. The same one I used to carry everywhere in the orphanage. My constant. My comfort. My friend, when the world felt too cold and too loud.

I stared at the photo, frozen, like I was meeting a version of myself I had almost forgotten. There was something haunting about seeing myself like that on a poster—like a lost pet or a charity ad. A child reduced to a question: Do you want me? As if my worth could be measured in a caption. As if my whole existence could be boiled down to that single line.

It made something stir inside me—something tender and sad and angry all at once. I didn't remember the picture being taken. I didn't remember posing or smiling. But there I was, frozen in time, holding that doll like it was the only thing in the world I trusted. And maybe, at the time, it was.

I traced the photo with my fingers, following the shape of my own face, my small hands wrapped around Raggedy Ann's soft body. My clothes were clean, my hair combed. It must've been taken during one of those early moments in the orphanage when they were trying to "place" us. Market us. I was a little girl asking the world for a home without knowing I was even asking. And here I was, years later, finding the evidence under a bed like a forgotten memory waiting to be found.

That poster said a lot more than it meant to. It said I had once been unwanted. It said someone had tried to make me desirable. It said my story started in a system that dressed children up and asked strangers to want them. But what it didn't say—what it couldn't say—was how that little girl had survived. What she'd carried. Who she had become.

And at that moment, holding that piece of paper, I didn't know whether to cry or to smile. Because somehow, even after all the abandonment, after all the screaming, after all the fear, I was still here.

Still me.

Still wanting to be wanted.

Still hoping that someone, somewhere, already had.

Taken

Why have you taken away my hopes and dreams?

Why do you hate me? You could never love me, it seems.

I just wanted a mother to tuck me in at night,

A mother who, if I was hurt, would fight.

Who loved me despite the color of my skin,

Whose love sometimes came from deep within.

Why do you hate me? What have I done?

Can't you see what I might become?

You've taken everything from me. What more can you take?

Dedicated to my adoptive mother, Anna RosaOrtiz

CHAPTER 2
THE UNWANTED PROBLEM

Without José in the picture, we were no longer wanted. The shift was instant, like a door slamming shut without warning. One day, we were part of a family—maybe not perfectly loved, but at least included—and the next, it was like we were just extra mouths, extra noise, extra weight. We went from being adopted children to burdens. That word burden was never said out loud, but it lived in every look Anna gave us, in every sigh when we walked into a room, in every slammed door and skipped meal. You can feel when you're no longer welcome. It hangs in the air. It hums in your bones.

We weren't allowed upstairs anymore. Not even to sit on the couch or pass through the kitchen like the others. It was like the rules had quietly changed, and no one told us—except with their eyes, their silence, their distance. The basement became our prison. Same circus wallpaper and the same twin beds, but now it felt smaller. Colder. Like the joy had been scraped out of it. What once felt like our space, our little world, was now where they sent us to disappear.

The only time we saw Anna was when she brought us food, which wasn't often. A paper plate. A slice of bread. Sometimes, leftovers scraped together without a word. She didn't come down to talk or check on us. She opened the door, left the food, and closed it behind her like we were something she needed to forget. We waited for her footsteps to fade before we moved. That's how much tension lived in the air.

Years passed. And when I say years, I don't just mean time ticking on a calendar—I mean years of growing up in silence. Years of learning how to shrink ourselves. Years of raising each other, of surviving without being seen. We got taller. Our voices changed. Our hearts hardened in places. But we stayed there, in that basement, tucked away like forgotten boxes in the dark.

Waiting. Enduring. Becoming strong in ways children should never have to be.

By the time I was six and Luis was five, we were old enough to go to school. It should've been a time filled with crayons, storytime, and playground laughter, but for us, it was different. We didn't have parents brushing our hair or making our lunches with love. Every morning, I played the role of "mama." Not because someone asked me to but because someone had to. It became routine, automatic, instinctual. I'd wake up early and start my quiet ritual—find his little clothes, help him slip his arms through his shirt, tie his shoes, and brush off the dust from the night before.

I dressed Luis, made him a peanut butter sandwich, and gave him half of mine. I didn't think twice about it. It didn't matter if I was hungry, too. He was smaller. He was weaker. He needed more. And he was all I had.

He wasn't just my brother—he was my responsibility, my comfort, my reason for being strong when the world gave us no softness. I would've given him anything just to see him smile. That was enough for me.

Luis had a lot of health problems and was constantly in and out of the hospital. I never knew exactly what was wrong—nobody explained it to me in a way I could understand—but I knew something wasn't right. His body was tired more often than mine. He'd run for a while, then sit down suddenly, clutching his chest or curling up without a word. And every time they took him away in an ambulance or walked him out the front door with a coat wrapped tight, I'd feel like the floor beneath me was giving out, like my whole world was disappearing one trip to the hospital at a time.

I had to protect him. That truth lived in me deeper than anything else. I had to make sure he was safe. From sickness. From strangers. From the cold. From Anna's rage. From this world that didn't seem to care whether a little boy with big brown eyes lived or died. I stood between him and everything I could, even if it meant standing alone. I didn't have armor, but I had love. And sometimes, love was enough to make me brave.

Even now, I don't know how I managed it all at six years old. But when you love someone that deeply, that completely, you just do what needs to be done. No questions. No rest. No complaints. Just a little girl playing mama because no one else would.

I would take every beating, every punishment just so he wouldn't have to. If I saw her rage building, I'd step forward. If something went wrong, I'd say it was me. It didn't matter if I was scared; it only mattered that Luis was safe. That was my only mission. My small body became a shield, over and over, and somehow, I learned to stand still even when everything inside me screamed to run. I'd bite my lip, close my eyes, and brace for it. If I could take it, then maybe Luis wouldn't have to feel it. That was the deal I made with life. That was the price of being the strong one.

Anna's abuse got worse. It didn't matter how quiet we were or how clean the room was. There didn't need to be a reason. Her anger came like weather—sudden, wild, and impossible to predict. She screamed at us like we had personally ruined her life. She pulled our hair until our scalps burned, yanking us across the room like rag dolls. And when her hands weren't enough, she used whatever she could get her hands on— extension cords that left long, raised welts; belts that snapped in the air like thunder; wooden spoons that cracked against our backs and arms until they broke in two.

But for some reason, she hated me the most. I could feel it every time her eyes landed on me—sharp, cold, almost disgusted. Like just my being there was an offense. And I never knew why. I never asked. I was too afraid of the answer, or maybe I already believed the worst. That I wasn't good enough. That I was too much. That my silence, my sadness, or just my face set something off in her that she couldn't control.

All I ever wanted was for her to love me. That's it. Just love. Just a soft word, a warm hand, a hug that didn't hurt. I wasn't asking for the world. I was just a little girl who wanted to be seen—not as a burden, not as a mistake, but as someone worthy of kindness. I watched her laugh with her own children. I saw the way she brushed Evelyn's hair, the way she kissed Juan's cheek. I wondered what made them lovable and what made me... not.

She never did love me. Not even a little. And as much as that broke my heart, it also made it stronger. Because even without her love, I still protected my brother. I still got up every day. I still held onto whatever light I could find.

And that—that love I gave even when I didn't receive it—was my power.

Innocence

A touch, a hug, a simple kiss—

Does his innocence even exist?

You trust someone with your life,

But in the end, they cut you with a knife.

They break your heart, they cause you pain,

They make you cry; they take away your sunshine.

No more dolls, no more playing,

Because your innocence was taken.

It was not given, but with this fear comes hope,

And you live life because you're driven, and you learn to cope.

Dedicated to Americo Burretto, a.k.a. Mikey.

CHAPTER 3
STOLEN INNOCENCE

One day, my entire world shattered. Luis had gone off to school. I was home; I had stayed back that day, sick, lying alone in the basement. My stomach hurt, my head was heavy, and the silence in the house was deeper than usual. It was the kind of quiet that makes you feel invisible, like the world had kept moving and left you behind. I lay curled on my bed, the circus wallpaper staring back at me, faded and peeling at the edges.

Then I heard footsteps on the stairs—slow, deliberate. Mikey, Anna's oldest son, came downstairs. He was a teenager, already taller than most of the adults in the house, and something in his eyes always made me uneasy. He stood at the bottom of the stairs, looking at me for a moment before speaking. "Lisa, it's time for your shower," he said.

I was six years old.

I didn't understand what was happening. His voice sounded normal, like any other day. I didn't think to question him. I just nodded. I was used to doing what I was told. Obedience had become a kind of survival. So I stepped into the shower like I always did. The water turned on, warm and steady, running down my small body. For a moment, it felt like nothing was wrong. Just another morning. Just another shower.

But something felt different. Off. I could sense it in the air, in the way the door didn't fully close, in the silence that wasn't empty but watching. A heaviness I couldn't name settled on my chest. My little hands trembled under the stream of water. I didn't know why yet. I just knew something in the world had shifted.

Innocence isn't always lost in one loud moment. Sometimes, it slips away in silence, in small, confusing pieces that don't make sense until years later. That day marked the beginning of a different kind of pain. One, I didn't know how to speak. One that would live in my bones, quiet and burning, for a long time.

I didn't understand it then. But I would carry it with me. And over time, I would learn to name it. To face it. To survive it.

Because even in the dark, I refused to let it be the end of my story.

Then, I heard the shower door open. Mikey stepped inside.

He was naked.

The only thing he wore was a single white sock with blue stripes. A strange, almost surreal detail—one that would stay etched in my memory far longer than anything else in that room. That sock would become a symbol of everything that didn't make sense. Everything that shattered.

"Don't look at me," he whispered. "I won't hurt you."

But I was frozen.

His voice wasn't calm; it was calculated. I didn't move. My breath caught in my throat, my body stiff like it had turned to stone. I was six years old, too young to understand what was happening but old enough to know something was terribly, terribly wrong. My heart pounded so loud I could hear it echo in my ears.

He tied the sock around my head, blindfolding me.

The world disappeared into darkness. I couldn't see anything. And somehow, that made it worse. Because I didn't know what was coming, I couldn't prepare. I couldn't protect myself. I stood there, trembling, the sound of water still running like nothing had changed, like the world hadn't just shifted on its axis.

Then he told me to reach for the soap.

But what I felt—it wasn't soap.

It was something else. Something that didn't belong in a child's hands. It was longer, harder.

It had hair.

I froze again, my small hand jerking back in confusion and dread. Mikey was breathing heavily. Each breath felt like a storm on the back of my neck, and I wanted to disappear, to dissolve into the water, to be anywhere but there. But I was trapped. At that moment, in that body, in that nightmare, I couldn't wake up from.

No screams came out. Just silence. Just fear. The kind that doesn't make noise but burrows deep into the soul and stays there for years.

What happened next doesn't need to be described to be understood.

What matters is this: something was stolen from me that day. Not just innocence. Not just safety. But the belief that adults protected children. That showers were just showers. That home meant home.

And yet I lived. I carried it. Somehow, I walked out of that bathroom. I kept breathing. I kept surviving.

Because even though he tried to break me, he didn't.

I am still here.

His hands gripped my small body.

Rough. Controlling. Unforgiving.

Then, he took what was not his to take.

There are no words that can ever fully describe what it feels like when your body is no longer your own, when you are used like an object, silenced by fear, pinned beneath something you can't fight or understand. Pain. Blinding, searing pain. It split through me like fire, so sharp and shocking it knocked the breath from my lungs. I wanted to scream, but I couldn't. My voice disappeared. It got stuck in my throat, wrapped in the same knot as my fear.

I bit my lips to keep from screaming, to keep from making a sound that might make it worse. But I couldn't stop the tears. They slid down my cheeks, silent and constant, mixing with the steam in the air and the water from the shower. I shook so hard I thought I'd fall apart. My little fingers clutched at nothing. My mind tried to float away, to leave my body, to go anywhere else, but I couldn't escape.

Then I felt something warm dripping between my legs.

Blood.

I didn't know how to make sense of it. All I knew was that it hurt inside and everywhere. That something sacred had been broken, something no child should ever have to understand.

When he was done, he whispered.

I don't even remember the words, only the chill they left behind. Maybe he said I'd be okay. Maybe he told me not to tell. Maybe he said nothing at all. It doesn't matter because the damage has already been done.

And there I was, naked, bleeding, blindfolded, and alone.

But I was still alive.

Somehow, I picked myself up off that shower floor. Somehow, I got dressed. I didn't cry out. I didn't run. I just moved, like a ghost of myself. Because when something like that happens, you don't always fall apart right away. Sometimes, you just go numb. You pretend it didn't happen. You bury it so deep even you start to wonder if it is real.

But it was.

And I would carry that moment with me for years. Not because I wanted to but because it had branded itself into my body, my memory, my soul.

Still, he didn't break me.

He hurt me, yes. He scarred me. But he did not destroy me.

And that... is where my story begins to change.

"You're a good little girl, Lisa. But don't tell my mom, or she'll send you back."

Those words echoed in my head long after he left. They weren't comfort; they were control. A warning wrapped in fake affection. I stood in that shower for an hour, scrubbing my skin raw. I rubbed until my arms burned, until the skin turned red, until the water ran cold. But I could never wash away what he did to me. No matter how hard I scrubbed, it stayed. Not just on my skin but deep inside me, like something lodged beneath the surface of my soul.

Anna knew. I think she knew.

She came down later to do laundry, her usual sharpness muted for a moment as she sorted through the clothes. I stood nearby, small and silent, trying not to tremble. She picked up a pair of my underwear and held it in her hand for a beat too long. There was blood. Right there. A stain no child should ever leave behind. She saw it. I know she did. She saw the way I limped. She saw how I flinched when someone walked behind me. But she never asked. She never said a word. She folded the laundry, tossed it in the basket, and walked away like nothing had happened.

She didn't care.

And maybe that was the part that cut the deepest—not just what Mikey did, but the silence that followed. The silence of a woman who was supposed to protect me. A mother who once called me pretty and made me dresses. Who now looked through me like I was invisible. Like I was too ruined to be worth saving.

From that moment on, the little girl inside me was gone.

Gone was the hopeful child who thought she'd one day be loved.

Gone was the girl who believed God would save her.

Gone was the softness, the innocence, the wide-eyed wonder. All of it evaporated in that one moment, stolen in the steam of a shower and buried in the folds of a blood-stained undergarment. What remained was something harder. Quieter. A shell trying to keep breathing in a house that had become a graveyard for trust.

On that day, I became a woman.

Not because I was ready. Not because I understood what that meant. But because trauma doesn't ask for your permission. It just takes. It shapes you before you're old enough to even hold the pieces. It turns little girls into survivors.

I was six years old.

And already, I had survived more than most grown women could ever imagine.

CHAPTER 4
A FALSE HOPE

We all loaded up in Anna's packed Volvo, all six of us crammed inside. The car smelled like old upholstery and stale crackers, the kind of scent that lingered no matter how many windows were rolled down. Bags were piled in the back, squished under legs, and pressed into laps, leaving little room to breathe. I sat in the backseat, squeezed between Juan and a suitcase that kept shifting every time we hit a bump. The seatbelt dug into my side, but I didn't say anything. I just stared out the window, letting the trees blur into long green streaks as we pulled away from the house that had never truly been home.

My thoughts were swirling with a fragile kind of hope. A hope I didn't dare say out loud because saying it made it real, and if it turned out to be false, I wasn't sure I could take that kind of heartbreak again. But still, it was there, flickering quietly like a tiny flame refusing to die.

Maybe Florida will be different.

Different from the cold basement.

Different from the silence. Different from the pain.

Maybe Florida will bring us happiness.

That word happiness felt foreign on my tongue, like something I'd read about in books or seen on TV but never truly held. I imagined sunshine, maybe palm trees, maybe mornings without screaming. Maybe beaches and smiles and people who didn't look at me like I was broken. Maybe Luis would get better. Maybe Anna would soften. Maybe I'd get to be a kid again, even if just for a little while.

I didn't know much about Florida, but I knew this: it couldn't be worse than where we were coming from.

So I closed my eyes, leaned my head against the cool glass, and let that hope live just for a little while longer.

We moved to a small town called Deep Creek, where the rich white people lived. Everything looked clean, quiet, and manicured—the kind of place where the lawns were always trimmed, and the houses looked like they had stories behind every window. It felt like we had crossed some invisible line like we didn't quite belong but were being allowed in barely. As we pulled into the driveway, my breath caught in my throat.

The house was beautiful.

Bigger than anything I had ever lived in. Maybe even anything I'd ever seen in real life. It stood tall and proud, with pale walls and wide windows that sparkled in the Florida sun. There was a porch with white railings, flower beds on either side of the front steps, and a yard that looked like it had been painted into place. My brown eyes widened as I took it all in, trying to believe that this might be our new home.

And then I closed them.

I closed them tight, like maybe if I shut out the world for just a second, I could make a wish that would actually come true. I sent up a silent prayer—not big or loud, just a whisper in my heart.

"Please, God... let me have a bedroom." That was all I wanted. Not toys, not clothes, not promises. Just a room of my own. A space where I could breathe. Where I could be a little girl again, if only for a few moments at the end of the day.

The moment the car stopped, everyone but Luis and I ran inside. They were laughing, calling out to claim their rooms, and slamming doors behind them like it was a race. I sat still for a second longer, my hand resting gently on Luis's shoulder. I looked at him. He looked at me. We didn't say anything, but we both knew. We were used to being last.

We waited, just like we always did, hoping there might still be space left for us—not just in the house, but in the life we were still trying to believe we deserved.

The movers had already brought in the furniture, and the older kids were rushing to claim their rooms like it was a competition. Their laughter echoed through the hallways, bouncing off the high ceilings and polished floors. There was excitement in the air for them, at least. Bags and boxes were being carried in and out, doors creaked open, and footsteps thudded across the hardwood upstairs. This was my new home. The thought felt heavy in my chest—too big to fully believe, too fragile to hold onto. I wanted it to be true. I needed it to be true. But part of me stayed cautious, waiting to see what would happen next.

Anna stepped out onto the porch, her face tight with annoyance like she had already expected more from us. She looked down at us from the top step and yelled, "Well, what are you waiting for? Grab your bags!"

Her voice cut through the warm Florida air like a whip-sharp and impatient, like the heat itself wasn't moving fast enough for her.

I didn't hesitate. I hurried to grab Luis's and my things, hoisting them up onto my small shoulders. The bags were heavy, but I had carried worse. I didn't flinch, didn't complain. I just bent down, wrapped my arms around what was ours, and followed behind her. Luis walked close beside me, his small hand brushing against mine every few steps, his eyes scanning everything like I was.

We walked toward the house like outsiders being allowed through a gate we didn't have the key to. I tried not to get my hopes up, but somewhere deep inside, I still clung to the wish I had made in the car— just a room. A place. A corner of the world that belonged to me.

And as I stepped over the threshold, crossing into this new chapter, I carried more than just our bags.

I carried all the weight of our story so far.

She led us through the house, down the hall, past the bedrooms one after another. I glanced through the open doors as we walked. Each room looked like something from a catalog: neatly made beds with colorful blankets, windows with soft curtains, posters already being hung on walls, and bags being unpacked with laughter and excitement. My heart thudded in anticipation. With every step, I silently pleaded; maybe this time we'd have a real room. Maybe this time we'd be wanted.

I held Luis's hand tighter, feeling the warmth of his little fingers wrapped around mine. His steps were quiet, like he, too, was holding his breath, hoping this new place might be different. Better. Maybe we'd get to wake up in a room with sunlight pouring through the window. Maybe we'd get to hang our clothes in a closet, put our toothbrushes by the sink, and have pillows that didn't smell like the past.

Finally, she stopped in front of a single door.

There was no excitement in her voice, no warmth in her gesture— just a sharp motion of her hand as she pointed.

"Go in there."

I hesitated.

Something about her tone, the way she didn't look at us, made me feel that old sinking feeling again. I gripped Luis's hand tighter, squeezing it like I could shield him from whatever was behind the door. My palms were sweating. My stomach twisted. But I had to know. I had to see it for myself.

I pushed open the door… and my heart sank.

It wasn't a bedroom. It was a utility room. A laundry closet. A converted space tucked into the far corner of the house with no windows and barely enough room for two twin mattresses pushed tightly against the walls. No circus wallpaper this time—just bare, beige walls and the hum of the water heater in the corner. There was no dresser. No light fixture, just a bulb hanging from the ceiling with a string to pull. The air was musty and heavy like the space itself hadn't been meant for people. Especially not children.

This was our room.

After everything, this was what we were given.

My eyes burned, but I didn't cry. I couldn't. Luis looked up at me, confused, hopeful, waiting to see how I would react. So I smiled at him— forced and fragile. I set down our bags and told him it would be okay.

But inside, something in me cracked because I knew.

We weren't here to be loved. We were just here, not to be seen.

It wasn't a bedroom.

It was a garage.

The moment I stepped inside, the cold concrete beneath my feet told me everything I needed to know. This wasn't a place meant for rest or comfort. It was storage. Forgotten space. A room made for things, not people. In one corner, there were six bags of trash piled high—some split open, the sour scent of old food and plastic filling the air. In another, three old bicycles leaned against the wall, their chains rusted, tires half-deflated, like ghosts from another life. The light overhead flickered, buzzing faintly, casting a dull yellow haze across the room.

The only thing on the floor was a thin, worn-out throw rug, so faded it was impossible to tell what color it once had been. It didn't cover the whole floor—just enough to fool the eye at first glance. Dust clung to everything. The air was stale and heavy with the scent of mold, gasoline, and something unnameable. And in that moment, every fragile hope I had built in the backseat of the car came crashing down.

Luis looked up at me, his voice small, full of confusion.

"Where's the bed, Lisa?"

I felt my throat tighten. That question hit like a punch. He still believed we were being given something—a chance, a home, a place to rest. I didn't want to break that for him. Not yet. I swallowed the lump in my throat and forced myself to speak.

"I don't know… I guess we have to make one."

As if on cue, Anna walked in.

No knock. No warning. Just her shadow filling the doorway, eyes flat and uninterested. She didn't even look at us—just tossed a single blanket and two couch cushions onto the floor like scraps thrown to animals.

"This is where you'll sleep," she said.

And then she turned to leave as if that was all there was to say like we didn't deserve more than that.

I hesitated.

Not because I didn't understand we weren't getting anything better but because I needed a second to hold it in. To stop me from crying in front of Luis. I looked at the blanket—thin and frayed, barely enough to cover one of us, let alone two. The cushions were stained, flat, smelling of smoke, and years of use.

This was our room.

This was how we were seen.

Not as children. Not as souls. But as things to be managed. Hidden.

But I didn't cry. Not then. I just bent down, spread out the blanket on the rug as best I could, and laid the cushions side by side. I told Luis it would be okay, even though I knew it wasn't.

Because, at that moment, I wasn't just his sister.

I was the only home he had.

"What if we need to use the bathroom?" I asked, my voice small but steady, hoping—maybe begging—for a shred of dignity, for the simplest form of humanity.

Anna didn't even pause.

"Knock on the door," she replied flatly. "If no one answers, go outside." And with that, she left.

No explanation. No second thought. She just turned on her heel and walked out, the door creaking shut behind her with a final thud. It sounded more like a prison door than the entrance to a house. Her words settled over the room like dust—cold, careless, final.

I stood there for a moment, staring at the door, trying to process what I'd just heard. Not even a key. Not even a promise someone would be listening. Just knock. And if we were ignored, like we often were, we were to relieve ourselves in the bushes. Like animals. Like intruders on someone else's property.

I turned to Luis.

He sat quietly on one of the couch cushions, his little hands resting on his lap. He didn't say anything, but his eyes spoke volumes. There was no fear in them, at least not the kind that showed, but there was confusion. Sadness. That innocent ache that comes when a child is starting to realize the world doesn't always make room for them.

He looked so small sitting there. So still. Like he didn't want to take up too much space. Like he already knew that space here came with conditions.

I wanted to say something to make him feel better. I wanted to tell him it was going to be okay. But all I could do was kneel beside him, gently place my hand on top of his, and sit with him in the silence.

Because sometimes, that's all we had.

Each other.

And a blanket on the garage floor.

CHAPTER 5
SURVIVING THE
UNTHINKABLE

I remember that year like it was yesterday. It was 1983, and Cyndi Lauper's "Girls Just Wanna Have Fun" was playing on the radio throughout Anna's house. That song was everywhere. It seemed to bounce from room to room, upbeat and full of life, like it had a heartbeat of its own. I could hear it spilling through the vents and cracks in the walls—loud, bright, impossible to ignore. It became the soundtrack of that season, even if it didn't belong to me.

I could hear Evelyn and Virginia singing the song, dancing around the house without a care in the world. Their voices floated through the air—high-pitched, cheerful, a little off-key—but full of that reckless freedom only young girls with love and safety know how to have. I couldn't actually see them, but I could hear them clearly from the garage, and I could just picture them, real outgoing, twirling in the living room, hair flying, socks sliding across the floor, laughing like nothing in the world could touch them.

And I wasn't angry, not at them. I didn't feel jealousy; I felt distance. Like I was watching a movie play out on the other side of a glass wall.

They were inside the life I had dreamed of, and I was out here, listening through the cracks, trying to gather pieces of joy that didn't quite belong to me. I'd close my eyes and imagine what it would feel like to dance with them. Just once. To be invited into the room. To have someone pull me by the hand, laugh with me, see me.

But at that moment, I was still the girl in the garage. Still the one on the outside. And yet, I memorized every word of that song. Not because it was mine but because it reminded me that fun was possible. That girls like me, somewhere, somehow, were having fun. And maybe, one day, I would too.

Meanwhile, Luis and I were in the garage, cleaning up the space that would become our new bedroom. Our adoptive mother, Anna, had decided—without discussion or apology—that the garage was where we would sleep. No explanation, no offer of comfort. Just a blanket, a couple of cushions, and the unspoken message: This is all you deserve.

It was cold and cluttered, filled with old boxes, broken lamps, deflated balls, stacks of dusty papers, and forgotten items that no one cared enough to sort through. Cobwebs hung like ghosts in the corners, and every step stirred up a little more dust. We sneezed, coughed, and rubbed our eyes, but we kept working. Because that's what we did. We made do. We turned whatever space we were given into something livable, even if it never quite felt like home.

As we cleaned, the upbeat music from the radio provided a stark contrast to our reality. Cyndi Lauper's voice filtered through the thin garage walls: "Girls just wanna have fun…" and for a moment, it felt like the whole house was dancing except us. We could hear the others—Evelyn and Virginia—laughing, stomping, singing at the top of their lungs.

The rhythm of their joy thumped overhead like a world we weren't allowed to enter.

But in the quiet corners of our garage, Luis and I tried to make the best of it. We folded the blanket carefully, propped the cushions side by side, and swept the floor as best we could with an old broom we found leaning in a corner. We made up games out of cleaning, out of organizing. We turned trash into treasure just to keep from thinking too much about what we didn't have.

We found small moments of joy in each other's company despite the circumstances—moments that felt like gold in a place that had none. A shared joke. A quiet giggle. The simple comfort of knowing we weren't alone in the world, even if the world didn't seem to want us.

We were kids with broken pieces, trying to build something whole out of the scraps we were handed.

And somehow… we did.

The garage was far from the cozy bedroom we had hoped for, but we did our best to make it feel like home. It wasn't easy. The concrete floor stayed cold no matter how many blankets we layered. The air had a permanent chill, even in the Florida heat, as if the room itself had never been meant to hold warmth. Still, we tried. We arranged our few belongings neatly—folding our clothes into careful stacks, lining up our shoes, and placing our toothbrushes in an old cup we found in one of the boxes.

Every little thing we did was an act of quiet resistance. A way of saying, We belong somewhere, even if it's here.

We tried to create a space where we could feel safe. A space where, when the door closed, we could let our guard down just a little. We whispered stories to each other at night, invented make-believe games, and traced invisible patterns on the ceiling to distract ourselves from the ache of being overlooked. Luis would sometimes draw little faces in the fog on the window, and I'd pretend they were visitors from a world where kids like us had real beds, real families, and real love.

The sound of Cyndi Lauper's voice and the laughter of Evelyn and Virginia echoed through the house, spilling into the garage like sunlight we couldn't quite reach. It was a reminder of the life we were now a part of, even if it felt distant and unattainable. Their joy felt like it lived on a different frequency—one we could hear but never truly join. We were there, technically under the same roof. But emotionally, we were in another country. One where survival came first, and childhood came second if it came at all.

Still, we held onto what we had. Each other. A blanket. A corner of a garage. And the unspoken promise that somehow, someday, things would be better.

Because even in the coldest places, hope has a way of finding a crack to grow through.

I began to clean up our new home. I moved slowly, sweeping dust into little piles, picking up stray bits of paper and broken objects like it mattered. Like if I cleaned it well enough, it might feel less like a garage and more like a bedroom. More like something we could actually belong to. I folded our clothes neatly, smoothed out the thin blanket, and placed our shoes by the wall, side by side, like it made a difference. It was okay, though. Because in my heart, I believed all of this was temporary.

One day, our mother would realize she was wrong for leaving us.

One day, she would come looking. One day, she would find us.

I clung to that belief like it was air. I imagined her walking through the door, arms open, tears in her eyes, saying she was sorry that she missed us, that she never meant to leave, that she had been searching all this time. In my mind, it played like a movie, over and over. That hope was the only softness I had to wrap myself in.

One day, we would be safe and happy again.

That thought was enough to get me through the long hours of the day, through the looks from Anna, through the coldness that wrapped around us every time the garage door shut. That dream of rescue, of reunion, of love was what carried me forward.

Luis and I went to sleep that night on couch cushions in the garage. No pillows. No nightlight. Just each other, curled under a thin blanket, our backs pressed close for warmth. The room was dark but not silent. I could still hear the radio upstairs. I could still hear the sound of laughter, distant and unreachable. I stared up at the ceiling, tracing the shapes of shadows, whispering promises to myself that I didn't dare say out loud.

And even though I was afraid, even though the cement beneath us was unforgiving, I closed my eyes and held onto hope.

Because sometimes, hope is the only thing a child has left.

Tomorrow, we will start school. And I wanted to make something quick to wear.

Somewhere in between those quiet, in-between moments of survival, I had learned how to sew just by watching Anna back in New Jersey when she was making me those beautiful little dresses. I would sit quietly off to the side, not saying a word, just observing her every move. I was fascinated by the way she transformed simple fabrics into lovely garments. Her hands moved with precision and certainty like she was casting spells with thread. And I absorbed every detail: how she measured, how she cut, how she folded seams just right. I watched with wide eyes, eager to replicate her techniques whenever I had the chance.

Whenever I did get clothing, it was usually older, worn-out pieces. Hand-me-downs. Discarded things no one else wanted. But I saw potential in them. Where others saw rips and stains, I saw an opportunity. I would cut them up, throw some paint on them, add a stitch here, a tuck there, and suddenly, they looked brand new. Or better than brand new.

They looked like me.

My creativity flourished in that small, quiet rebellion. I experimented with different styles and wild designs, never worried about rules or trends. I always had a unique sense of style, partly because I no longer cared about fitting in or conforming to what other kids thought was "normal." I didn't have the luxury of trends. My fashion choices became a form of self-expression. A way to show the world that even in the middle of hardship, I still had a voice. That I still had beauty inside me. That I was more than what I had been through.

As a child, sewing and redesigning old clothing was more than just a hobby. It was a necessity. It was the only way I could have something "new" to wear. The only way I could walk into school with even a thread of dignity. I took pride in my creations, even when no one noticed, even when others laughed or looked confused. Because each piece I made—each altered dress, each painted sleeve, each uneven hem—was a testimony of my resourcefulness and determination.

This early experience... taught me something powerful: that even when the world gives you scraps, you can still make something beautiful. That you can take what's broken and build something that is entirely your own.

With sewing and crafting, I laid the foundation for the skills I now carry as an adult. Today, I can make things with ease—drawn not from formal training or fancy tools but from the raw lessons I learned during those formative, survival-driven years. Looking back, I realize now that my ability to create and innovate was born out of necessity—born out of a deep, pressing need to express myself when words didn't feel safe or welcome.

It became my way to cope with the challenges I faced. A way to reclaim some sense of power in a world where so much had been taken from me. It gave me something beautiful to focus on when life felt anything but beautiful.

Sewing became more than just a skill. It became a metaphor for my life.

Taking what was old and worn and transforming it into something new and beautiful—that was my truth. That was my superpower. That was my art. Where others saw scraps, I saw possibility. Where others saw damage, I saw a blank canvas. Even when I was a little girl in that cold garage, piecing together dresses from discarded fabric, I was already shaping my identity stitch by stitch.

I always had a different sense of style, and not because I was trying to stand out. I dressed the way I did because I no longer cared about fitting in. I didn't dress for approval. I dressed to survive. I dressed to express. My style was the voice I wasn't allowed to use, the freedom I hadn't been given. It was how I claimed space in a world that tried to make me small.

Maybe that's why, as an adult, I can still create with such clarity and confidence because I've been doing it since I was a child. Because back then, creating was the only way I could have something new to wear, something to call my own. It wasn't just about clothes—it was about identity. About dignity. About saying, "I am still here. I am still worthy. I am still me."

I started school the next day, but I wasn't just beginning classes like the other kids. I was also going to have to attend speech therapy. I had developed a stuttering problem—one that didn't come from birth or genetics but from the abuse I was enduring while living with my adoptive mother, Anna, and her son, Mikey.

I think one of the reasons I had to go to speech therapy when I started school was because I began stuttering really badly. It didn't happen all at once. It crept in slowly as the fear and trauma built up inside me. As I held in more and more pain, it was like my words didn't know how to come out anymore. They got stuck in my throat, tangled somewhere between what I wanted to say and what I was afraid to feel.

The abuse I endured from Anna and Mikey and the constant fear I lived in had silenced something inside me. My speech was horrible. I couldn't even talk properly. The words were there, but they stumbled out, stuttered, and stuck like they were trying to push through a wall I couldn't see. It was a constant struggle. I'd try to speak and feel the eyes on me—the impatience, the confusion, the quiet judgment.

The stuttering made me feel isolated and frustrated. It separated me from the other kids in a way that I didn't know how to explain. I felt like I was trapped in my own mouth, like my voice was betraying me. And at that age, when all you want is to be understood, to belong, to feel normal, it was devastating.

It was as if the trauma I experienced was manifesting in the most necessary part of my life: my ability to speak. My ability to say, "I'm here." And yet, I couldn't say it clearly. The words came, but not easily. Not freely.

But I still showed up. I went to speech therapy, even when it was hard, even when I was embarrassed, even when I didn't want to speak at all. Because something inside me refused to give up, that space, small as it was, became a place where I could begin to reclaim something. A place where I could work, slowly, gently, to overcome a challenge I didn't ask for but one I was determined not to let define me.

And in that room, with the speech therapist guiding me word by word, I started to heal just a little. Not all at once, but enough to feel like maybe my voice was still mine.

I learned techniques to manage my stuttering, and over time, I gradually began to gain confidence in my ability to speak. It didn't happen overnight. It was a slow and painful process, filled with frustration, embarrassment, and moments when I wanted to give up completely. But each small victory—saying a full sentence without stuttering, raising my hand in class, reading out loud—felt like climbing a mountain.

Speech therapy became more than just a class. It became a lifeline. A place where I could start to believe that I didn't have to stay silent forever.

Despite the abuse and the difficulties I was still facing at home, I persevered. I was determined to express myself. Determined to be heard. Because deep down, I knew my voice mattered, even if it shook, even if it stuttered.

Every word I forced out was an act of courage.

Outside, the next day was long. It was hot. The Florida sun beat down with no mercy, and the school felt too big, too loud, too unfamiliar. I was placed in the fifth grade, though everything about me felt too small—my body, my voice, my spirit. Looking back, I realize now that fifth grade was the beginning of my real troubles. The beginning of a new kind of battle. One that would push me in ways I couldn't have prepared for.

At home, I was learning to survive.

But at school, I was about to learn how deeply the world could wound a child already carrying more than most grown people ever would.

I don't remember my teacher's name, but I do remember one of the only friends I made that year—Wade Gingrich. His name has stayed with me, even when so much else from that time has blurred. I wonder where he is today. I wonder if he ever thinks about those afternoons we shared, those small, meaningful conversations that meant the world to me.

Wade and I talked about everything and anything—school, dreams, the weird lunches they served in the cafeteria, things we didn't tell anyone else. With him, I didn't feel strange. I didn't feel broken. He never laughed at my stutter or made me feel small. He just saw me. And in a world that constantly tried to erase me, that meant everything.

He was one of the only people I trusted.

Then, one day, I did something that changed everything.

We were sitting quietly in class during free time, and I grabbed a piece of paper. My hands moved before I even knew what I was doing. I didn't write—I drew. Not shapes or cartoons or the happy little pictures kids are supposed to make. I began to draw the truth. My truth. I sketched out what life really looked like for me—the garage, the couch cushions, the crying, the bruises, the silence. The faces of people who hurt me and the shadows that lingered long after.

It wasn't pretty.

But it was real.

And for the first time, I wasn't hiding. I wasn't pretending. I was telling the truth in the only language I felt safe using: art. That drawing became a mirror I didn't even know I had the strength to hold up. And once it was on the page, there was no taking it back.

Something had begun.

I sketched a picture of Mikey and what he did to me. I don't know why I did it. Maybe because I needed someone—anyone—to see what I had been through. Maybe because the weight of the secret had grown too heavy, and I needed to lay it down somewhere, even if just on paper.

Maybe I was hoping, deep down, that someone would finally save me. That someone would see it and say, "You don't have to carry this alone anymore."

I showed the drawing to Wade.

He looked at it, and at that moment, everything changed. The moment his eyes landed on the image, his face twisted with something fierce: anger, disbelief, maybe even grief. I'll never forget that look. Like the innocence of childhood had been yanked away from him, too, just from seeing what I lived with. He didn't hesitate. He snatched the paper from my hands and ran straight to the teacher without saying a word.

The next thing I knew, I was standing in the principal's office. My heart pounded in my chest, my palms sweaty, my stomach in knots. The room was cold and too quiet. The principal held my drawing in his hands, studying it in silence. His eyes moved slowly over the page, his brow furrowed, his lips pressed in a tight line. I stood there, frozen, feeling small, exposed, and terrified.

Then he picked up the phone.

I already knew who he was calling.

Satan herself. Anna.

A few moments later, she arrived: heels clicking against the tile, purse swinging, voice bright as always. She walked into the office with her usual fake smile and that hollow laughter that made my skin crawl. Her whole body was a performance like she was starring in a show where she played the perfect, misunderstood mother.

"Oh, I have no idea why Lisa did this!" she chuckled, shaking her head.

"Kids and their marginations!" she laughed again, louder this time like the whole thing was some silly joke.

But no one else was laughing.

And I stood there, watching her spin lies while my truth sat in the principal's hands: raw, undeniable, and finally, finally visible.

But when she glanced at me, her eyes darkened.

That smile she had worn like a mask for the principal disappeared in a flash, replaced by something colder, hard, sharp, venomous. She didn't have to say a word. I knew what was coming. I felt it in my bones. The warning was in her stare alone. It was the kind of look that told me: You'll pay for this later.

As soon as we left the school building and the last set of adult eyes was no longer watching, her grip tightened around my arm. So tight I could feel the blood rush away from the skin beneath her fingers. She yanked me toward the car with such force that I stumbled, trying not to cry out. But crying would only make it worse. So I swallowed it.

She pinched me all the way to the car, her nails digging deep into my skin—little crescent moons of rage carved into my arm. Her teeth clenched, her lips drawn tight, her fury simmering just beneath the surface. She didn't speak. Not a word. But the silence screamed louder than any yelling ever could.

We drove home in silence.

Not the kind of silence that brings peace, but the kind that coils in your stomach and twists. The kind that presses down on your chest like a weight. The radio stayed off. The air felt suffocating. I stared out the window, trying to distract myself with passing trees, mailboxes, anything but the burning in my arm or the storm I could feel building beside me.

When we pulled into the driveway, I braced myself.

My fingers gripped the edge of the seat, and I held my breath as she turned off the ignition. For one small second, I wished time would freeze. That maybe if I sat still enough, quiet enough, I could delay what was coming. But I knew better.

This wasn't just punishment.

This was payback for telling the truth.

She yanked me out of the car with such force my feet barely touched the ground. Before I could even catch my balance, her hand flew across my face—open palm, full swing. The slap landed with a crack so loud it echoed in my ears. My vision blurred instantly. A hot, stinging pain spread across my cheek, and for a moment, everything around me went fuzzy.

I held my cheek, swallowing back my sobs. I didn't cry, not out loud. I had learned not to. Tears only fueled her. Tears made her go further. So I bit the inside of my lip hard, tasted blood, and kept quiet.

She dragged me into the kitchen by my arm, her nails biting into my skin. The linoleum floor blurred beneath my feet as I stumbled behind her. She shoved a chair back from the table and forced me into it like I was nothing more than a disobedient pet. I sat there, small and trembling, the world spinning slightly as the heat from the slap throbbed against my face.

I sat there for what felt like forever.

The ticking of the clock. The hum of the refrigerator. Every sound felt loud and sharp, like the air was electric with her rage. I didn't look at her. I didn't speak. The weight of her fury pressed down on me, heavy and suffocating. I couldn't run. I couldn't hide. I could only sit there and brace myself for whatever came next. Finally, she leaned down.

Her face was so close I could feel the heat of her breath against my skin. I could see the hate in her eyes—not disappointment, not anger. Hate. Pure and deliberate. Inches from my face, her voice dropped into a whisper, but it was the kind that cuts sharper than any scream.

"It never happened."

The words were ice.

My lips trembled. My whole body shook. I opened my mouth, but nothing came out. I couldn't speak—not from fear, but from the way her words struck like chains, wrapping around my throat and locking down my truth.

She said it again, slower this time, her voice like poison in my ear.

"It. Never. Happened."

In that moment, something in me broke.

Not loudly. Not visibly. But deep inside, a piece of me curled inward—wounded, silenced, made to question everything I knew to be real.

And yet, somewhere in the quietest part of my spirit, I knew it did happen. No matter what she said. No matter how many times she tried to erase it.

It happened.

And one day, I would say it out loud again.

But for now, I stayed still. I stayed quiet.

And I survived.

I whispered back. My voice was barely audible, more breath than sound. But I said it.

"It did happen."

The words shook as they left my mouth, but they were mine. Quiet. Fragile. But real.

Because I knew the truth.

It did happen.

Mikey did hurt me.

And she—Anna—didn't care. She knew. And she chose silence. She chose him. She chose the lie.

The weight of that truth - that betrayal, crushed me in a way I can't fully explain. It was like the air had been ripped from my lungs, like the world had lost all color. I couldn't stay in that kitchen one second longer. I couldn't sit under the gaze of the woman who let it all happen.

So I ran.

I ran outside, past the car, through the yard, and into the trees that stood like quiet witnesses to everything I was too small to carry. I didn't stop to look back. I didn't think. I just moved, fueled by something ancient and primal inside me that screamed, get away, get away.

I ran until the ground turned to mud beneath my feet, until the branches scratched my skin, until my legs ached and my chest burned.

Finally, I collapsed onto the cold, damp leaves, the earth welcoming me like it knew my sorrow. I fell to my knees and let it all out.

I screamed.

I screamed until my throat was raw, until the sound was less like a voice and more like a wound breaking open. I screamed like I wanted the trees to carry my pain into the sky.

Like I wanted the world to hear what no one in that house would.

I pulled at my hair, trying to make the pain inside match something I could see on the outside. I scratched at my arms, desperate to feel something other than the ache in my chest. I cried until my body had nothing left to give—no more tears, no more sound, no more fight.

And at that moment, surrounded by fallen leaves and branches, I felt both completely shattered... and strangely free.

Because I had told the truth.

And even if no one else would carry it with me...

I knew it was real.

And that mattered.

Looking back, I realize I still do this as an adult. I still run—maybe not through the trees anymore, but in other ways. I still disappear when things hurt too much. I still find myself searching for silence when my soul is screaming. Because the trauma never really leaves. It doesn't vanish just because time has passed. It settles into your bones, into the fabric of who you are. It waits, quiet and patient, until a moment of weakness, of fear, of memory... and then it rises.

Trauma is real.

It isn't just something you survive. It's something you carry.

By the time I returned home that night, it was dark. The sun had long since dipped behind the trees, and the air was heavy with the weight of everything I had just lived through. My clothes were damp from the earth, and my face still streaked with dried tears. My body ached with exhaustion, but I kept moving back to the only place I had left: the garage.

I slipped inside quietly, the door creaking just enough to make my heart race. And there he was—Luis curled up on the cushions, eyes wide and shining with fear. The moment he saw me, he sat up fast, his little hands clutching the blanket we shared like it could protect him from whatever he imagined had taken me away.

"Lisa... I thought you weren't coming back."

His voice cracked on the last word. And something inside me shattered all over again.

I dropped to my knees beside him, pulled him close, and wrapped my arms around him so tightly I could feel the rhythm of his heartbeat against my chest. I held him like I could shield him from everything—Anna, Mikey, the pain, the world.

"You're all I have, Luis," I whispered into his hair.

And I meant it with every piece of me.

"You're all I have."

And in that small, cold garage, surrounded by darkness, trash bags, and broken things, we held each other. Two kids. Two survivors. Two hearts still beating in spite of it all.

"I would never leave you."

I whispered it into his ear like a vow, not just for that night but for every night that would follow. No matter how dark the days became, no matter how cold or cruel the world felt, I would be there. For him. Always.

I asked if he had eaten.

"No," he said, his voice small and tired.

I sighed, trying to hide my worry behind a soft smile.

"Don't worry. You'll eat at school tomorrow. Please don't cry. Everything's going to be okay."

But it wasn't.

It never got okay.

Not for a long, long time.

Things only got worse.

I started getting suspended from school all the time. Not because I was bad—not really—but because I was broken, angry, silent one day, and explosive the next. I carried too much pain and not enough words. The teachers didn't understand me. The system didn't protect me. So they punished me instead.

And that meant staying home.

But staying home didn't mean staying inside because Anna wouldn't let us in.

She locked the doors—all of them. Even the garage. Even the one place we thought we could hide. And just like that, Luis and I were shut out, literally. Cast aside like we didn't exist, like we were just too much to deal with. So, we spent our days sitting outside in the grass. Hungry. Confused. Abandoned.

With nowhere to go.

At first, we just waited. Sat there, side by side, watching the door, hoping it might creak open.

Hoping maybe Anna would remember we were children. That we needed food. Shelter. Mercy. But she never came.

As time passed, we stopped waiting.

We started finding ways to make the hours go by. We talked about silly things. We made up stories. We searched for shapes in the clouds. We played games with sticks and rocks. We counted ants on the sidewalk. We built little forts out of branches and leaves. Anything to make the day feel less empty, less painful, less forgotten.

Because when the world turns its back on you, you learn how to make something out of nothing.

And that's what we did.

We made each other laugh, even with growling stomachs.

We shared everything—thoughts, fears, dreams, crumbs.

We survived another day. Together.

We wandered the neighborhood, not because we were looking for trouble, but because we had nowhere else to go. Nowhere safe. Nowhere warm. We walked the streets like shadows, quiet and watchful, slipping between yards like whispers. We snuck into backyards, cutting through hedges and climbing fences, our eyes always scanning for something— anything we could use. Food. Water. Shelter. We weren't stealing for fun. We were surviving.

We took bikes left outside—the ones with loose chains or rusty handlebars, bikes that looked forgotten. Whatever we stole, we hid in the woods behind the house, beneath a pile of branches we called "the stash." It was our secret place, the only space we had control over. A place where no one could yell at us or lock us out. It felt like freedom, even if just for a moment.

One day, we walked up to a house we hadn't seen before and tried the back door.

It was unlocked.

We looked at each other—Luis's eyes wide with fear, mine wide with desperation—and stepped inside, our hearts pounding so loud it felt like the walls could hear them. My breath caught in my throat, adrenaline racing through every part of me. I knew it was wrong. I knew we could get caught. But I was hungry. Luis was hungry. And hunger makes you brave in ways you don't want to be.

The first place I ran to was the kitchen.

My hands moved fast, automatic, frantic. I grabbed a bag from under the sink and started filling it with whatever I could find: cookies, cereal, Coke, sandwich meat, crackers, peanut butter, and a pack of gum. I didn't stop to read the labels or think twice. I just stuffed it all in, breathing hard, heart thudding in my chest like a drum. I didn't know when the family would come back. I didn't care. We just needed to eat. We just needed something.

And in that moment, standing in a stranger's kitchen, hands shaking as I filled a plastic bag with stolen food, I didn't feel like a criminal.

I felt like a child trying to survive.

Luis found two Game Boys with games tucked away in a drawer. His face lit up like Christmas morning. For a moment, it was like we were just two kids again—excited, laughing, wide-eyed at a treasure we never expected to find. We didn't stay long. We knew better than to push our luck. We slipped out the back door, clutching our bags tight, and ran as fast as we could through backyards, through the trees, until we reached our hiding spot in the woods.

We tore into the food like animals. We drank the Coke straight from the cans—cold, fizzy, and perfect. We ate the cookies, one after another, stuffing our mouths between giggles. We devoured the sandwich meat, not even bothering with bread. We were starving, and for the first time in what felt like forever, we were full. Full bellies. Full hearts. Just for that moment.

It was wrong, and we knew it. We weren't proud. But when you've been hungry long enough, guilt takes a back seat to survival. At least we weren't hungry anymore.

The next day, we went back to check on our stash, our little sanctuary. I had forgotten about the animals. I should've known. The scent of food in the open woods was like an invitation. They had gotten to everything. The cookies were shredded. The meat was gone. Wrappers scattered everywhere like confetti from a party we never got to enjoy.

But not our Game Boys.

They were still there, tucked under a piece of plastic tarp we'd dragged out of the trash weeks before. So we sat there, cross-legged on the forest floor, dirt smudged on our faces, sun beaming through the trees, and played. For hours. Game after game. Escaping reality one stolen pixel at a time. In those little screens, we could win. We could have control. We could be anyone but the kids locked out of their homes with no food, no love, and no place to belong.

We thought we were getting away with it.

But people started noticing.

The neighbors started to whisper. They saw us—two kids, sitting in the yard day after day, locked out of their own home. They saw us riding around late at night, unsupervised, looking lost and worn down. Someone must have put the pieces together.

HRS was called.

Child Protective Services.

And the story we had tried so hard to keep quiet—our truth, our hunger, our pain—was about to come to light.

The cops came. Their uniforms looked sharp, their voices steady and professional, but I couldn't tell if they actually saw us—really saw us. They asked questions. They took notes. They walked through the house like they were looking for something specific, but I don't think they found it. Or maybe they didn't want to. I stood there, heart racing, eyes shifting from their faces to Anna's, hoping—praying—that this time would be different.

And when they left, I thought... maybe. Just maybe someone would save us.

But they didn't.

The door clicked shut behind them, and the sound felt louder than any scream, like a verdict. Like hope being locked out once again.

Anna turned to me and Luis with that cold fire in her eyes, her smile long gone. "Go to the garage."

And I knew what was coming.

My stomach dropped. My legs went numb. But I walked anyway, back to that place that was supposed to be our room but felt more like a punishment every day. She followed behind us, not in a rush. Her rage was methodical.

Then came the extension cord.

She beat me until my legs bled—long, stinging welts that opened beneath the rubber, the pain sharp and hot. I clenched my teeth and forced my body to stay still. I refused to scream. I refused to give her the satisfaction. I wouldn't let her hear the sound of my pain. I took every lash in silence, eyes burning, fists clenched, heart pounding in my ears.

When it was over, I stood up.

My legs were shaking, but I made my way to the bathroom. I cleaned myself up with quiet hands and wiped away the blood the best I could. I put my clothes back on like armor, straightened my shoulders, and walked back to Luis like nothing had happened.

I sat down beside him, pretending I was okay.

And that's when I finally let the tears fall.

Not loud, not dramatic—just quiet streams down my face. The kind of crying that doesn't need sound to break you. The kind that feels like release and collapse all at once. And Luis didn't ask what happened. He didn't need to. He just sat beside me, silent and close.

And once again, we survived. Together.

I knew I was in the wrong for stealing. I wasn't proud of it. I wasn't trying to pretend like it was okay. But to beat me like that? To make me bleed for wanting food? For trying to survive? I couldn't understand it. I was a child. I made a mistake, but didn't every child? What I did didn't deserve that.

And then, out of nowhere, I started laughing.

It bubbled up from deep inside me, sudden and sharp, catching even me by surprise. Luis looked at me, wide-eyed and confused.

"Why are you laughing?" he asked, his voice soft, his face still puffy from holding back tears.

I looked at him, still laughing through the pain, through the bruises, the silence, and the rage boiling just beneath the surface.

"Because we won't get dinner tonight… but at least she didn't find our Game Boys and bikes."

For some reason, I found that funny.

Don't ask me why.

Maybe it was the absurdity of it all. Maybe it was the only power I had left—to laugh when everything else hurt too much to feel.

Luis stared at me for a second, then slowly smiled. It was small, uncertain, but real. And just like that, for a fleeting moment, we weren't two discarded kids in a garage. We were survivors who still had something—anything—that was ours.

That night, as I lay on the cold garage floor, the pain still fresh in my legs, I stared up at the cracked ceiling and wondered:

How long could we keep going like this?

How many more beatings would there be? When would someone finally see us—not as trouble, not as shadows, but as children who needed saving?

The silence didn't answer.

So I closed my eyes, held the blanket tighter, and told myself:

"At least she didn't find the Game Boys."

Sometimes, small victories were the only ones we had.

I knew I was in the wrong for stealing. I wasn't proud of it. I wasn't trying to pretend like it was okay. But to beat me like that? To make me bleed for wanting food? For trying to survive? I couldn't understand it. I was a child. I made a mistake, but didn't every child? What I did didn't deserve that.

And then, out of nowhere, I started laughing.

It bubbled up from deep inside me, sudden and sharp, catching even me by surprise. Luis looked at me, wide-eyed and confused.

"Why are you laughing?" he asked, his voice soft, his face still puffy from holding back tears.

I looked at him, still laughing through the pain, through the bruises, the silence, and the rage boiling just beneath the surface.

"Because we won't get dinner tonight… but at least she didn't find our Game Boys and bikes."

For some reason, I found that funny.

Don't ask me why.

Maybe it was the absurdity of it all. Maybe it was the only power I had left to laugh when everything else hurt too much to feel.

Luis stared at me for a second, then slowly smiled. It was small, uncertain, but real. And just like that, for a fleeting moment, we weren't two discarded kids in a garage. We were survivors who still had something—anything—that was ours.

That night, as I lay on the cold garage floor, the pain still fresh in my legs, I stared up at the cracked ceiling and wondered:

How long could we keep going like this?

How many more beatings would there be? When would someone finally see us—not as trouble, not as shadows, but as children who needed saving?

The silence didn't answer.

So I closed my eyes, held the blanket tighter, and told myself:

"At least she didn't find the Game Boys."

Sometimes, small victories were the only ones we had.

What would it feel like to have a real family?

I used to ask myself that all the time. Not out loud, but in those quiet moments when everything was still, when the house had gone silent, and I was lying on the cold garage floor with Luis breathing softly beside me. In the dark, my imagination became the only place I could go where love still seemed possible.

What would it feel like to come home from school and have a snack waiting for us?

Not a stolen cookie or a scraped-together sandwich, but something made with care. Something with our names on it. Something that said, "I thought of you today." What would it be like to walk through the front door and hear someone ask how our day was? To see someone's eyes light up just because we were home?

What would it feel like to hear someone say, "I love you"?

To hear those words and believe they were true. To feel them in the way someone held your face, or tucked you in at night, or made sure your favorite shirt was clean. "I love you"—the simplest words, and yet the most impossible thing for us to imagine. Because we never heard them.

Anna never said she loved me. Not even once.

Not when she gave me a dress. Not when I cleaned the house. Not when I tried to be good. Not when I cried. Not when I bled.

She never looked at me with softness in her eyes. Never reached for my hand just to hold it. Never hugged me without force. She fed me only when it was convenient. She spoke to me only when there was something to correct. She raised me, yes, but she didn't love me. Not the way a mother is supposed to.

And even as a little girl, I knew something was missing.

I didn't have the words for it then.

But I felt it. In every unanswered question, every door shut in my face, every silent meal. I felt it in the empty space where love was supposed to live.

Why?

That question echoed in my chest more times than I could count.

Why didn't she love me?

Why couldn't she see how badly I wanted to be loved?

Didn't she notice the way I tried to help, the way I stayed quiet, the way I looked up at her with hope in my eyes, hoping she might soften, even just once?

Even now, as an adult, I still wonder.

I still feel that ache deep, familiar, quiet, but persistent. That longing for love. For acceptance. For someone to choose me, not out of obligation, but out of desire. Out of genuine care. I've lived so many years since that little girl in the garage, but part of her still lives in me—still waiting, still wondering, Will I ever stop feeling this way?

I don't know.

Sometimes, healing feels like chasing a shadow. You can see it, feel it, but never quite catch it. But I do know this:

Anna was tired of us.

Tired of the responsibility. Tired of pretending. Tired of keeping up the lie. We had become too much. Not just our needs but our existence.

We were reminders of everything she wanted to avoid. So she did what she always did when faced with something she couldn't control.

She got rid of it.

She needed a break.

So, she sent us away to Puerto Rico.

No explanation. No warning. No tearful goodbyes or promises to visit. Just another decision made without our voices. Another message sent loud and clear: You're not wanted here.

And just like that, we were gone again. Packed up. Shipped out. Passed along like baggage too heavy to carry.

But what she didn't know was this:

We were stronger than she thought.

And no matter where she sent us, we still had each other.

In His Eyes

In his eyes, I saw hope for a better day,

Love and devotion through caring in every way.

I never knew how affected he was by the hurt in our life,

I never took into consideration his pain or strife.

I never understood the depth of his love,

I never knew he would risk it all just to get a hug.

He was just a boy in so much pain,

And from the look in his eyes, I thought God forgot his name.

Dedicated to my little brother, Luis Acker.

By Lisa Acker

CHAPTER 6
NOWHERE TO BELONG

So here we were, back in Florida, back at Anna's house—a place Luis and I never wanted to return to. Every step toward that front door felt heavier than the last. The walls, the smell, the air—it all carried memories we had tried to leave behind. But we had no choice.

Where else could we go?

We were just kids, and the world wasn't made to catch kids like us. We thought maybe—just maybe—DCF would step in again. Maybe they'd see the bruises. Maybe they'd hear our story. Maybe they'd finally send us to another foster home—one with warmth, with kindness, with real beds and food that wasn't earned through silence.

But that's not what happened.

Because Anna had legally adopted us.

On paper, she was our mother. In the eyes of the law, that made her permanent. That made her family. That made her immune to the truth we lived every single day. The system saw signatures and documents—not the bruises, not the cold dinners, not the locked doors. Not us.

In reality, she never treated us like her children.

Not even close.

We weren't her sons and daughters. We were her responsibility. Her burden. Her secret. Her labor. Something she had once chosen and now regretted. We didn't get hugs or "I'm proud of you" or "How was your day?" We've got rules. Punishment. Silence. Survival.

And yet here we were again—back in that house, back in that garage.

Back under her roof but never truly under her care.

Luis and I started school again, going through the motions like ghosts in someone else's life.

We woke up each day in the same garage, sleeping on the rough carpet with one thin cushion between us and the cold, unforgiving concrete. There were no blankets unless we managed to hold onto one from the night before. No pillows. No warmth. Just the hum of the water heater, the creak of the garage door, and the quiet knowledge that we were not wanted.

We weren't allowed inside when Anna and her "real" children were home.

That rule was unspoken but always enforced.

So we spent most of our time outside. On the porch. In the yard. Wandering the neighborhood. Sitting under trees, drawing in the dirt with sticks, or watching other kids ride their bikes home to places where someone cared they were coming back. We tried to get by. We tried to make it feel normal, even when it never was. But things only got worse.

Anna's daughter Evelyn was kind to me. She'd talk to me sometimes, ask how I was doing, and offer a smile or a scrap of food when no one was watching. It wasn't much, but it meant the world. Her kindness felt like a lifeline, like proof that someone in that house still had a heart.

But Virginia?

Virginia made it very clear she didn't want me there.

She never hit me. She didn't have to. Her words were sharp enough. Her looks were colder than the garage. She'd roll her eyes when I walked by, whisper under her breath, and slam doors behind me just to remind me I was in the way. She made sure I knew that I was the other. That I didn't belong. That I wasn't family.

And no matter how quiet I was, how careful I tried to be, it was never enough to keep the peace.

So Luis and I stuck together.

Two shadows in the same storm, trying to stay warm with nothing but each other.

Whether she disliked me personally or simply resented me for being different, I'll never know. Maybe I reminded her of something she didn't want to see. Maybe it was jealousy. Or maybe it was just easier to blame me than to face whatever was broken inside that house. Whatever the reason, Virginia never missed a chance to make me feel like I didn't belong.

One day, she became furious over something—I can't even remember what. Maybe I used her brush, or maybe I borrowed something of hers without asking. It could've been anything, really. In that house, the line between harmless and punishable was always shifting. There were no warnings, no conversations—only explosions.

All I remember is her storming outside, face twisted with rage, fists clenched, her voice already rising before she even reached us.

Luis and I were sitting in the grass, just trying to stay out of the way. The sun was out. The yard was quiet. For a brief moment, we were simply being kids, plucking blades of grass and talking about nothing. Trying to forget where we were and who we were living with. Trying to pretend we had a moment of peace.

Then she came.

And the air changed.

We weren't allowed inside the lanai, where everyone else sat comfortably laughing, eating, and talking like they belonged to a family that actually functioned. That space was off-limits to us, like every other part of the house that held warmth. So Luis and I stayed outside, like we always did, sitting in the grass, pretending not to hear the clinking of silverware or the bursts of laughter coming from behind the screen door.

Then she came.

Virginia.

She walked out with a storm in her eyes and hate in her mouth. I could feel it before she even said a word. There was no warning. No reason that made sense. Just that same fury she always seemed to reserve for me.

She grabbed the water hose, turned it on,

and started spraying us. Full pressure. Ice cold.

The water hit my chest, my face, and my legs, soaking through my clothes in seconds. Luis let out a yelp, startled and shivering, but I didn't move. I couldn't. I just sat there, frozen, staring at her, unable to believe this was really happening.

"This is what they did to people like you back in the day," she spat, her voice thick with disgust.

She wasn't just being cruel.

She was being hateful. Deliberate.

"I don't even know why my mom keeps you here," she said, walking closer, still holding the hose like a weapon.

"You're embarrassing to this family. You're dirty. You're nothing."

Did it hurt?

Of course.

More than the sting of the water, more than the chill that clung to my skin—it was her words that hit the hardest. Her voice, her hate, her belief that we didn't belong. That I wasn't worth kindness. That I was less than human. And the worst part? Deep down, part of me believed her. Because when you've been treated like nothing long enough, it starts to feel like the truth.

But I didn't cry.

Not in front of her.

I just wrapped my arms around Luis and whispered that it would be okay, even though I wasn't sure it ever would be.

Because sometimes, the only thing more powerful than hate is holding on anyway.

More than anything, it confirmed what I already felt deep in my bones: I didn't belong.

Not in that house.

Not in that family.

Not in the version of life everyone else around me seemed to live so effortlessly.

That night, Luis and I ran away again.

There was no dramatic goodbye. No packed bags. Just a quiet decision, a shared look, and a burst of courage born from pain. We waited until the house was still, until the moon was high, and the wind didn't feel so sharp. Then we crept out into the night with nothing but the clothes on our backs and a fire in our hearts to get as far from Anna's house as we could.

We made it to a neighbor's house—not because we trusted them, but because we knew what they had: bicycles. Two of them. Just sitting there in the open, unlocked, waiting like they had been placed there for us. We didn't hesitate. We got on and started pedaling. No lights. No plan. Just movement.

We rode all the way from Deep Creek to Port Charlotte, Florida.

If you know the area, you know that it's at least a 35- to 45-minute drive by car.

By bike?

It felt like forever.

Our legs burned. Our bodies ached. The streets stretched on endlessly, and the night seemed to grow colder with every mile. But we didn't stop. Not once. Because we knew what we were riding away from, and even if we didn't know where we were going, anywhere felt better than the place we'd left behind.

For the first night, we slept on the beach.

We found a patch of sand away from the crowds and curled up together, using each other's body heat to stay warm. The waves crashed nearby, soft and steady, like lullabies meant for someone else. The stars above us blinked quietly, and for a few hours, we weren't kids in danger. We were kids at rest. Not safe, but freer than we'd been in a long time.

I sent Luis to Walmart with the few dollars we had scraped together to grab a tent—anything that could give us a little shelter from the night. I watched him walk away, small and determined, and it broke something in me that he even had to do that. No child should have to learn survival this young. But we did.

The next night, we found an unfinished house under construction and slipped through the framing to sleep inside. There was no door, just wooden beams and concrete flooring, but it was dry, and it felt safer than the open beach. For that night, it was home.

After that, we discovered a small mobile home sitting vacant on a quiet lot. It looked abandoned. The curtains were drawn, and the grass was high. We checked every day to make sure no one came by. When no one did, we stayed. We slept there for a while—nervous but grateful. We cleaned it as best we could, made a little corner of ours, and tried not to leave too many traces behind. It wasn't much, but it gave us a roof. And that was everything.

Eventually, we ended up at the mall, wandering between food courts and store entrances, looking for warmth, maybe kindness, or just someone who might notice we needed help. That's where I met Gary. He was white, soft-spoken, and friendly in a way that made me both cautious and hopeful. He seemed to want to help. After living on the streets for a week,

Luis and I were exhausted. Our bodies were sore, our clothes dirty, our stomachs always empty. But it was Luis I worried about most.

He was never as strong as me.

Not physically, not emotionally. He still had his childhood innocence, and I clung to that with everything I had. I was just trying to protect it. Trying to protect him.

Gary took us to his parents' house in North Port. It was a quiet neighborhood, with well-kept lawns and wind chimes hanging from porches. But the moment we stepped inside, I felt like I didn't belong. I could tell this was temporary. I could tell I had to be careful.

When Gary's parents came home, I had to hide in the closet.

I crouched in the dark, knees pressed to my chest, heart pounding. I listened to voices, footsteps, and the sound of cabinet doors opening and closing. I stayed quiet. I stayed invisible.

Gary gave us food, but only a little.

Just enough to get by.

Not enough to feel full.

Not enough to feel safe.

But still more than we had the night before.

And in that moment, even a scrap of kindness felt like something holy.

At some point, Luis decided to go back to Anna's house.

He was tired—tired in the way only a child without a home can be. I think he needed the illusion of security, even if it came with pain. He needed a routine, a bed he knew, a door that locked. Even if it also came with screaming, silence, and bruises. It was a choice between two types of suffering, and he chose the one that felt familiar.

So, Gary and I dropped him off at the corner down the street.

I remember watching him walk away, his little shoulders hunched, his backpack bouncing against his spine.

He didn't look back.

And I didn't call out.

We both knew the words would hurt more than the silence.

As for me, I knew Anna wouldn't care where I went.

Not really. Not ever.

She wouldn't call the cops. She wouldn't ask neighbors. She wouldn't drive around looking for me. I wasn't her daughter. I was her problem. And my absence was her convenience.

So I stayed with Gary.

He was the only person who had fed me in days. The only one who had looked at me without disgust. The only one who hadn't raised his voice hadn't raised a hand. That alone made him feel safe. Or safer, at least. At night, I slept in his bed. Tense at first. Always waiting for a shift in tone or a trap to be sprung.

But he was gentle.

And I didn't know what love was—not really.

But in my mind, maybe this was it.

Maybe this was what it felt like to be wanted. To have someone notice when you were cold. To have someone share their food without expecting you to earn it. To lie next to someone and not feel fear crawling up your spine.

It wasn't perfect.

It wasn't even permanent.

But at the time, it was something.

And for a girl who had spent her life being unwanted, something felt like everything.

He started giving me alcohol—drink after drink, night after night. At first, I didn't understand what was happening. I thought it was just something older people did, something you were supposed to do to feel accepted, to feel wanted. And I let myself believe that this was care. That him handing me a bottle was some twisted version of love. The warmth that spread through my chest was affection. That the fog in my head was comfort.

But looking back, I know now that it wasn't.

It was manipulation.

It was control.

It was exploitation.

He took advantage of me, and I let him.

Not because I wanted to.

Not because I liked it.

But because in my childhood mind, I thought I had to.

I thought this was survival.

Because what else was there?

I had no one.

No family to run to.

No home that felt safe.

No real childhood to cling to. That had been stripped from me long ago.

I had already been through things that made me feel broken before I ever met Gary. So, by the time he came along, I had stopped expecting anything different. I had stopped expecting kindness to come without a cost. I didn't know what boundaries were. I didn't know how to say no. I didn't even know if I was allowed to.

So I accepted it.

I felt disgusting, but I buried it deep inside. I told myself it didn't matter. That it was better than being cold and hungry, that maybe this was the price you paid to be wanted. That may be, this was just what love looked like for girls like me.

Because, at the end of the day, I just wanted to be loved.

Even if it wasn't real. Even if it hurt.

So, I stayed at Gary's house for a few weeks. While he went off to school like a normal teenager, I stayed behind. I didn't go to class. I didn't have a place to be. I had no ID, no schedule, and no one checking in. I was invisible.

I would walk up the street to the store and steal whatever I needed—clothes, deodorant, soap, toothpaste, a toothbrush. Not because I didn't want to ask but because I had learned that asking meant owing. And I had already paid too much.

Every day was just about getting by.

Surviving in silence.

And trying not to lose what little of myself I had left.

I had started my period back in Puerto Rico, so I needed things—pads, tampons, pain medicine—all the small, quiet necessities a girl's body demands, whether her life is stable or not. No one was going to buy them for me. No one even asked if I needed them. So I did what I had always done: I took care of it myself. I stole them.

I even grabbed some small things for Luis, just in case I ever saw him again. A pack of socks. A new toothbrush. Some snacks. It was habit by now—thinking about him, looking out for him even in his absence. He was the only thread that tied me to something innocent, something good. Taking care of him was the only thing that made me feel like I still had purpose.

To be honest, I didn't care if I got caught.

I was so used to being on my own.

Used to being hungry.

Used to surviving however I could.

There wasn't any fear left. Just motion. Just instinct.

It didn't matter anymore.

And then it happened.

I finally got caught.

I was walking out of the store with a few stolen things tucked into my coat when a hand touched my arm—firm but not violent. I looked up and saw the security guard. He didn't yell. He didn't drag me. He just told me to come with him.

And the strange thing is, I wasn't even scared.

I didn't fight it.

I didn't try to run.

I didn't cry or explain, or make excuses.

If anything... I felt relief.

Because, for once, I knew where I was going.

The detention center.

It was predictable. Structured. There would be food. A bed. A roof. I wouldn't have to hide in closets or steal tampons. I wouldn't have to keep pretending I was okay.

I think the stay was 25 days—maybe 31. I can't remember exactly. Time blurred.

But for once, I didn't have to survive alone. For once, someone else decided where I would sleep.

And in a twisted way, that felt like peace.

But I knew that for at least that long—those 25, maybe 31 days—I'd have a roof over my head. I'd have a bed that didn't sit on concrete. I'd have food in my stomach without having to steal it or earn it with silence. And most importantly, I would be safe.

Safe from people using my body.

Safe from Anna's beatings.

Safe from sleeping in the woods or in abandoned houses with Luis, watching over him like a second mother, terrified that something would happen to him while he slept.

For the first time in a long time… I could rest.

I could close my eyes at night without fear of crawling up my spine.

I didn't have to listen for footsteps.

I didn't have to plan an escape route.

I didn't have to be anyone but tired.

And I was okay with it.

I wasn't angry. I wasn't even sad. I was tired.

And this—this was the closest thing to peace I had known in years.

Looking back now, I can see how much of my life has been a cycle. One long, heartbreaking loop of hope and heartbreak.

First, I was in the orphanage after my real mother lost us to her addiction. She couldn't take care of us, no matter how much I wanted her to love me. I never even really knew her, just the stories. The image of who she might've been.

Then, I was placed with Anna, believing—hoping—that maybe this was it. Maybe she would be the mother I needed. Maybe I was finally going to have a home. But she wasn't. She was the beginning of another kind of pain. A more intimate kind. A betrayal wrapped in the disguise of adoption. She wasn't a mother. She was a lesson in survival.

And then… I ran.

Over and over again.

Every escape felt like freedom. But it was always temporary because there was never anywhere safe to land. Never anyone to catch me. So I just kept running—from pain, from rejection, from the crushing silence of being unwanted.

But in that detention center... for just a moment... I stopped.

And for the first time, I breathed.

And each time I ran, each time I was let down, pushed away, or betrayed, I lost more of myself.

Piece by piece.

Quietly.

Without ceremony.

Like parts of my spirit were being chipped away and scattered along the road behind me.

By this point, my innocence was gone. That wide-eyed little girl who used to whisper prayers into the darkness, who dreamed of being loved, who believed in family—she was fading. I couldn't find her anymore. I didn't have time to grieve her. I was too busy surviving.

My heart was turning cold.

Hard.

Angry.

There was a fire inside me now, one I didn't ask for. One that burned through sadness and replaced it with rage. Not loud, screaming rage—but the quiet, pulsing kind. The kind that settles into your bones. That tells you to never trust again. That dares anyone to try to get close.

I had been used. Tossed aside. Ignored.

And all of it had started to shape me into someone else.

I was becoming someone I didn't recognize. A whole new Lisa.

Not the girl who drew with crayons.

Not the girl who waited on the porch for a kind word.

Not the girl who still believed that love might save her.

Lisa didn't cry.

She didn't flinch. She didn't beg.

She fought.

She stole.

She survived.

Because when the world stops being gentle, you either break or you become harder than the world that broke you.

Innocence

A touch, a hug, a simple kiss—

Does this innocence even exist?

You trust someone with your life,

But in the end, they cut you with a knife.

They break your heart,

They cause you pain,

They make you cry; they take away your sunshine.

No more dolls, no more playing,

Because your innocence was taken.

It was not given.

But with this fear comes hope,

And you live life because you're driven, and you learn to cope.

Dedicated to Americo Barretto, a.k.a. Mikey

CHAPTER 7
A TEMPORARY ESCAPE

We were on our way to Puerto Rico.

As Luis and I sat on the plane, a flight attendant pinned little plastic wings onto our shirts as if that somehow made us special. She smiled brightly, her voice high and cheerful, as if this small gesture could turn the entire day into an adventure. But I wasn't fooled. I looked down at the cheap plastic and saw it for what it was: just another symbol of pretending. Did I feel special? Not even close.

Those wings didn't mean safety. They didn't mean love. They didn't mean home. They were a costume piece in a story someone else had written for us. I didn't feel excitement at that moment; I felt dread, uncertainty, and an ache in my stomach that had nothing to do with hunger.

A cart rolled down the aisle, offering snacks—peanuts, cookies, and Coke. The metallic clink of the wheels on the floor matched the rhythm of my heartbeat: fast, anxious. Everyone else on the plane seemed calm, even happy, like this was just a regular trip. But for Luis and me, this wasn't a vacation. It was another chapter in a story we didn't ask to be part of.

My little hands moved quickly, stuffing at least ten packs of peanuts into my underwear.

I didn't care who was watching. I didn't think about whether it was right or wrong. My body moved on instinct. I had learned by then that you take what you can when it's offered because you don't know when you'll get it again. The moment the peanuts hit my lap, I started sliding them under my shirt, into my waistband, hiding them the only way I knew how. They scratched against my skin and made me uncomfortable, but that didn't matter. Hunger had a louder voice than shame.

I looked at Luis, his face pressed to the window, eyes wide as he stared down at the clouds. Maybe he was dreaming. Maybe he thought things would be better in Puerto Rico. I didn't say anything to break that illusion.

Sometimes, I envied his ability to still hope.

But I was already preparing for the next time we'd go hungry. The next locked door. The next time, no one cared.

Ten packs of peanuts weren't just snacks.

They were insurance.

They were in control of a life that had offered us none.

And I held onto them like they were gold.

I just knew we wouldn't be allowed to eat much once we got there.

I had learned to predict it by then—to feel it coming like a storm just over the horizon. Food was always rationed like it was a privilege, never a right. I didn't know what Sylvia would be like, but I knew what it meant to be sent away, and it never meant comfort. So I kept those peanuts hidden like treasure. I sat stiffly in the plane seat, feeling them shift inside my clothes every time I moved. They were uncomfortable, sure—but they were mine. And I'd made sure we'd have something to eat later, even if it was just a few mouthfuls of salt and crunch.

Luis took a sip of his Coke, his big, beautiful eyes looking at me with quiet gratitude.

He didn't say a word, but he didn't have to. His eyes always spoke more than his mouth ever could. There was so much trust in that gaze. So much love. Even after everything, even through all the pain and—

She took us to her home, where she led us to a real bedroom with real beds.

Can you believe it? A real bed

Not a couch cushion. Not a patch of carpet in a garage. Not the cold ground beneath the stars. But actual beds, with mattresses, sheets, and pillows, smelled like clean laundry. Luis and I looked at each other like we had stepped into another world. It felt almost too good to be true. We set our things down slowly, cautiously, as if they might disappear if we moved too quickly.

We took in our surroundings with wide eyes. The room had a window that let in real sunlight, a dresser with drawers that opened without sticking, and even a small fan that whirred softly in the corner. For the first time in what felt like forever, we had our own space. A door that closed. A bed that didn't belong to someone else.

But even in that comfort, the ache of unfamiliarity settled in quickly.

Everyone around us spoke Spanish, fast and fluid, like music we couldn't quite understand. Words swirled around us, full of laughter and conversation we weren't part of. And just like that, we were outsiders again. Aliens in a place that looked like paradise but felt like another layer of distance.

Sylvia knew English, and she seemed kind enough in her own way. But I didn't want to be around her. I didn't trust kindness. Not anymore. I had learned that smiles could hide sharp things. That hospitality didn't always come from love. And I was tired of attaching myself to people who would eventually send us away.

So, once again, it was just Luis and me against the world.

We clung to each other in silence, making sense of the strangeness by staying close, our bond the only thing familiar in a place that buzzed with difference.

The next morning, Sylvia took us to school.

I remember the building—its concrete walls, open hallways, the warm air thick with the scent of ocean salt and sun. But what struck me most was the silence I was suddenly trapped inside.

Nobody spoke English.

Not the teachers. Not the students. Not the kids whispering and giggling in the courtyard. I sat in the classroom, unable to understand a word, my body there but my mind stranded. It was like being invisible all over again—seen but not understood, present but completely alone.

The girls stared at me, laughing amongst themselves.

They didn't say anything directly—not at first—but I could feel it. The side-eyes. The snickers. The way their hands covered their mouths just before a burst of giggles. I already felt out of place, like I was dropped into a world I didn't belong to. And to make matters worse, Anna had cut my hair so short I didn't even have a bob—just a tight, curly Afro that I hated.

It felt like she had taken one more piece of me.

I sat in the classroom, feeling every glance, every whisper. I tried to shrink in my seat, to disappear, to make myself invisible. I kept my eyes low, chewing on the inside of my cheek, pretending not to notice how out of place I looked.

I watched the other girls—how they carried themselves, how they tossed their hair and smiled like they belonged in the center of things. They had long, thick black hair, sleek and straight, shining in the sunlight.

Their clothes were polished, crisp, and bright, perfectly fitted. Their shoes looked untouched—brand-new as if they had just come out of a box that morning.

And then there was me.

Curly, short hair.

Big brown eyes.

Honey-colored skin.

Cheap, hand-me-down clothes.

Nothing about me blended in. Nothing about me looked polished or new or chosen. I felt like a mistake in a picture-perfect scene. Even the way I sat felt different—stiff, too careful, too aware of myself. I could feel the space between us, the line drawn in silence that said, You are not one of us.

And I wanted to cry.

But I didn't.

Because I'd already learned that tears didn't fix anything.

They just made you a bigger target.

So I sat still.

And I kept breathing.

And I reminded myself, At least Luis is here somewhere.

Even if no one else saw me... he did.

I didn't belong.

I never did.

Not here, not there, not anywhere that promised safety but delivered shame. I was always the outsider—the one with the wrong clothes, the wrong accent, the wrong everything. I tried to keep my head down, to make myself small, to coast through those first few days without attracting too much attention.

The first week was tolerable.

I kept to myself, did what I was told, watched everything, and said little. I floated on the surface, avoiding waves.

The second week was manageable.

The stares didn't sting as badly. The loneliness settled into something dull and familiar. I thought maybe I could ride it out—keep my head low, protect Luis, and count the days until it was over.

But by the third week, everything cracked wide open.

I found myself fighting on the playground.

It wasn't planned. It wasn't smart.

But it was inevitable.

A Puerto Rican girl came at me—loud, fast, filled with the kind of anger that kids who've never had to fight for survival don't understand. I don't even remember what she said. I just remember her hand grabbing my shirt, my fists grabbing her hair, and me swinging—swinging at her face like I was fighting every face that ever hurt me.

Then rip.

She snatched off my top mid-swing.

And suddenly, I wasn't fighting anymore. I was exposed.

The breeze hit my skin, and I froze.

That's when I realized I had no shirt on.

No bra—not that I needed one yet.

But still—there I stood. Open. Bare. Vulnerable.

Everyone could see that I had nothing.

Nothing to cover me. Nothing to protect me. No armor. No backup. No one to shield me from their eyes.

I felt the heat of humiliation burn through me like a fire I couldn't escape. It wasn't just physical exposure—it was spiritual. Emotional. That moment stripped away whatever thin layers of dignity I had left.

Everyone stared.

And I stood there, bare-chested and breathless, the crowd's laughter and whispers crashing over me like waves. I wasn't just ashamed. I was humiliated.

And in that moment, a new kind of anger was born.

I yanked my shirt back on and ran home. My heart was pounding so hard I could barely breathe, but it wasn't from the fight—it was from shame. From the eyes. From the laughter. From the feeling of being seen in a way, no child should ever be seen.

I was furious.

Furious at her.

Furious at the world.

Furious that no matter where I went, I was always the one on the outside.

Why did they hate me? What had I done?

I wasn't loud. I wasn't rude. I didn't try to take up space. I just wanted to exist quietly and peacefully. But that was always too much to ask. I had already been through enough in Florida. The beatings. The silence. The fear. I had already survived monsters in the dark.

And now I had to fight just to exist here, too?

I hated it.

Every hallway. Every classroom. Every face that looked through me like I didn't belong. I was tired. So tired of trying. Tired of holding it together. Tired of pretending like I was okay.

And then, to make matters worse, my body turned on me, too.

I got my period.

I was almost thirteen.

No one told me what to expect. No one gave me a guide, comfort, or supplies. There was no woman to turn to. No mother. No aunt. Just me.

The only person I could tell was Luis.

And what could he do?

I stuffed rags in my underwear to stop the blood. Stiff, rough pieces of old fabric folded over and over again, praying they'd hold long enough to get through the day. I was terrified someone would notice that I would leak. That someone would laugh. That I'd be humiliated all over again.

I felt desperate.

Alone.

Trapped.

Like even my own body was betraying me. Like I had nowhere to go. No one to lean on. No safe space to grow into the young woman I was becoming.

And so, I did what I always did.

I endured.

In silence.

In pain.

In secret.

And for the first time, I started to feel something else: suicidal.

It crept in quietly, like a shadow I didn't notice at first. Not loud. Not sudden. Just a dull ache, like a fog that settled over everything. I'd sit in silence for long stretches, staring out at nothing, feeling the weight of everything. The constant movement, the endless survival, the lack of love, of safety, of belonging—it all started folding in on me. I was only thirteen, but I already felt like I'd lived a thousand lifetimes filled with pain.

Despite everything, I picked up Spanish quickly.

I had a sharp mind, even when my heart was tired. I listened, absorbed, and repeated words under my breath until they stuck. Teachers noticed. Some classmates did, too. But still, I didn't make any friends. Not real ones. No one I trusted. No one who saw me. I had Luis, and thank God for that. But I wanted more. I wanted someone my own age to talk to. To laugh with. To feel normal with.

And that need made the silence around me feel even louder.

Sylvia barely paid attention to me, which, at first, honestly, seemed like a blessing. No rules. No hovering. No screaming matches. Just space. But after a while, the space became too quiet. Her indifference felt like erasure. I wasn't sure if she even remembered I was there some days.

And then... I started noticing things.

Sylvia was a loose woman, especially for her age.

Men came and went at all hours—older men, some of them gray-haired and wearing cologne too strong for the humid air. She would welcome them in with bright lipstick and low necklines. I saw the way they looked at her. I heard things through the walls. I watched her sometimes from the staircase—not in judgment, but in a strange kind of disbelief.

And I told myself, I hope I never end up like her.

Not because I hated her but because I saw something hollow in her eyes. Something desperate. Something performative. She wasn't loved either—just used in different ways than I had been. And I feared that might be my future, too. A body instead of a soul. A woman who gave and gave but never received real care in return.

I was spiraling.

I hated my life.

I hated how I looked.

My hair. My skin. My body. Everything about me felt wrong. Unwanted. Misplaced. I didn't feel beautiful. I didn't feel like a child. I didn't feel like I belonged anywhere on this earth.

I was only thirteen, and I already felt like I had no one.

So, one day, I went upstairs, knowing Luis was outside.

I moved slowly, quietly. My feet are heavy on the stairs. I wasn't sure what I was going to do exactly, but I knew I needed to be alone. I knew something in me was screaming for escape. I just wanted the noise to stop. The aching to stop. Everything to stop.

I opened Sylvia's dresser. And there they were. Three bottles of pills. I will never forget their colors; one bottle was green, and the other two were white.

The pills sat in a little bottle on the bathroom counter—small, chalky, unassuming. I didn't know exactly what they were. I didn't care. All I knew was that they looked like they could make everything stop. The noise. The memories. The ache in my chest. The endless days of being unseen, unheard, unloved.

I grabbed all three, then went searching. I found two more bottles under the sink.

Different shapes and different names, but all pills.

I brought them to the kitchen, poured myself a big cup of juice, and sat at the table like I was having an afternoon snack.

Then I started swallowing them—one by one, handful after handful. I didn't pause. I didn't think. I just kept going. The juice made it easier. I wanted it to be easy. I didn't want to taste the bitterness. I didn't want to feel anything.

That's when Luis walked in.

His feet scuffed the tile, and I looked up.

His face went pale, all the color draining as he realized what was happening. He was just a kid, but even then, he knew.

He knew this wasn't pretend.

He knew something was wrong.

He knew he was watching his sister disappear.

"Please don't tell," I begged him.

My voice cracked as I said it. I wasn't angry. I wasn't scared. I was just… tired. So tired. My eyes searched his face, silently pleading for him to just let me go. To let it be quiet. To let me rest.

And for a while, he didn't.

He stood there, frozen. Shocked. Maybe hoping I was joking. Maybe hoping it would just stop on its own. But then I felt it—the heaviness. My body started to sink. My eyes fluttered, and I couldn't keep them open. The world around me blurred like watercolors left out in the rain.

I guess he called Sylvia.

The next thing I remember, I was in the backseat of her car.

I was half-conscious, drifting in and out of awareness. The seatbelt pressed into my chest. The world whizzed by outside the window in streaks of color and light.

She kept yelling, her voice panicked and high: "Luis, don't let her close her eyes! Keep her awake!"

But I didn't want to be awake.

I wanted silence.

I wanted release.

I wanted the pain to stop—not just from that day, but from every day that had come before it.

My body was giving up, but inside, a small voice still whispered. It wasn't loud. It wasn't strong. But it said,

"Not yet."

I wanted to die.

That wasn't a passing thought or a dramatic cry for help. It was a quiet, deep ache that settled in my bones. It had built up over time, layered on by every betrayal, every slap, every night spent wondering why I wasn't good enough for someone to stay.

And to this day, I still wonder... Why didn't God take me?

Why did I wake up? Why, after all I'd been through, was I still here? I had begged—prayed—for it to end. Not out loud, not in front of anyone. But in the deepest part of myself, I had cried out to something bigger than me: "Please, let me go."

I woke up in a hospital bed.

The lights were too bright. The sheets too stiff. The smell of antiseptic clung to everything. And the moment I opened my eyes, a wave of pain crashed over me—not physical, but emotional.

The pain of waking up was worse than the pain of wanting to die.

I had hoped—prayed—that God would take me. I had offered up my life as a surrender. Not because I was weak but because I was exhausted. I had already been through enough.

I hated my life.

There was no sugarcoating it. I hated the pain. I hated the silence. I hated the pretending.

I resented my real mother.

Not just for leaving but for never coming back.

Why didn't she ever come back for me?

Why did she leave me to suffer like this?

I didn't ask to be born into chaos. I didn't ask to be passed around like luggage no one wanted to claim. I didn't ask to be broken. I just wanted someone to love me. To fight for me. To stay.

I wanted to disappear.

Instead, I spent a month in that hospital.

A full month in sterile white walls, being watched, being evaluated, being reminded that I was still here, whether I wanted to be or not.

I had almost died.

Thinking about it now, it still hurts. It still stings in that tender place inside me where the child version of me still sits, waiting for something different. Because at thirteen, I truly believed there was nothing left for me.

No future. No hope. No softness. Just survival.

When I was finally discharged, Sylvia took me home.

She didn't say much in the car. The silence between us was heavy, awkward, full of all the things she didn't know how to ask, and I didn't know how to explain.

She acted strange for a few days.

Quieter than usual. Maybe scared. Maybe guilty. Maybe just confused. Whatever it was, she kept her distance. And I was fine with that.

I spent time with Luis, like always. He was my anchor. My constant. My reason. We played games. Watched cartoons. Told jokes.

Pretending everything was fine.

Because that's what I did best, pretend.

Pretend I wasn't shattered.

Pretend I didn't want to leave this world. Pretend like waking up wasn't the hardest part of my day.

But inside, I still carried the weight of that question:

Why didn't God take me?

And slowly, somewhere deep down, another question started to whisper:

If I'm still here... maybe there's a reason.

We played and watched TV, and for a little while, it felt almost normal. Luis would laugh at cartoons, and I'd laugh, too—even if just to make him feel safe. And for the first time, I fully understood what was being said around me. Spanish wasn't foreign anymore. It was sinking into me, sentence by sentence. I could follow conversations. I could understand the jokes. I was finally catching up with the world around me.

But then I overheard something I wasn't meant to hear.

Sylvia was on the phone. Her voice was low, hushed, and urgent. I had gotten good at listening without being seen, at hearing things no one thought I could understand.

She was on the phone with HRS. They were coming for me.

And in an instant, my body went cold.

I knew what that meant. I had heard those letters before.

DCF. HRS. CPS.

Different names, same story.

It meant being taken.

It meant being thrown into another stranger's home, another bed I didn't choose, another house filled with rules and expectations, and the risk of abuse waiting around every corner.

I was about to be sent away.

I couldn't breathe. I couldn't think. All I could feel was that pull in my chest, the magnetic fear of being torn away from the only thing that kept me grounded: Luis.

I didn't want to leave Luis.

He was my heart. My reason. My anchor in every storm.

I didn't want to go to another home, wear another fake smile, or call someone else "Mom" who didn't love me.

I didn't want to be used and abused again.

So, I ran.

No time to plan. No map. No money. Only the clothes on my back.

I slipped out quietly, heart pounding in my ears, lungs burning with every step. I didn't look back. I didn't have a destination. I just knew one thing with crystal clarity:

I didn't want to go back into the system.

I didn't want another man taking advantage of me.

I didn't want to be another name on another folder.

I didn't want to feel unwanted, unloved, disposable.

So, I ran for my life.

Not toward anything but away.

Away from a future I had already survived once.

And I didn't know where I would land.

I just knew I had to try.

I just wanted to disappear. I wandered the streets as night fell, searching for somewhere safe to sleep. Every shadow looked like a threat. Every passing car made me flinch. I kept my head down, walking with no real direction, just trying to stay invisible. The air got colder as the hours passed, and the streetlights cast long, lonely shadows across the pavement. My stomach growled, but I ignored it. I was used to hunger. What I wasn't used to was being completely alone, not knowing if I'd make it through the night.

I found a small spot behind a store, grabbed a piece of cardboard, and laid it down like a bed. It wasn't warm. It wasn't comfortable. But it was hidden, and that was enough. I curled up on my side, tucking my knees into my chest, trying to make myself small. I stared up at the stars, peeking through the spaces between the buildings, and pretended I was back in Florida, hiding in the woods with Luis. Back when things were hard but familiar. Back when I wasn't alone. I thought about the sound of his laugh, the way we used to make up games to pass the time. I missed him with every part of me.

Then I closed my eyes.

I didn't expect to wake up. Not really. A part of me was okay with disappearing, with fading into the background of a world that never made space for me. But life had other plans.

The next morning, I woke up to police officers standing over me. Their voices were stern but not cruel. I blinked up at them, the morning light harsh against my face. My throat was dry, and my body sore from sleeping on the ground.

They asked for my name. I told them. My voice cracked, quiet but steady. And just like that, I was taken back to Sylvia.

I thought that meant my time in Puerto Rico was over. Maybe someone had realized I didn't belong there and that I would finally be sent back to Florida or somewhere else far away from all of it. But it wasn't over. Not yet.

Sylvia called HRS again. This time, they didn't ask questions. This time, they didn't wait. They came quickly, paperwork in hand, and just like that, I was gone. Not back to Luis. Not back to the house, I knew. But to somewhere completely unfamiliar.

This time, they took me away for good.

I was placed in a new foster home. The woman who took me in was nothing like Sylvia. She was a religious fanatic—strict and controlling. Her house was spotless, her tone clipped and cold. There was no warmth in her eyes, no softness in her hands. Her rules were gospel, and there was no room for questioning. Church five times a week. No excuses. No exceptions. It wasn't a home; it was a correctional facility with a Bible on every surface. And once again, I found myself adjusting, surviving, shrinking. Because that was the only way I knew how to exist.

No TV. No playtime. Just prayer. That was the rhythm of the house—morning, noon, and night. Every hour accounted for with scripture or silence. At first, I thought, Okay, at least it's not like before. At least no one was screaming at me. At least I had a bed, meals, and clothes that didn't smell like mildew. I tried to convince myself this was better. That maybe, just maybe, this kind of strictness was a weird form of care. But then I noticed something.

She kept taking me to her neighbor's house.

A truck driver. A grown man. Always alone. Always watching me too closely. He would offer me a seat on the couch, his eyes scanning me like I was being sized up for something I didn't ask to be part of. I tried not to look at him, tried to sit still, tried not to breathe too loudly. But every time I was brought over, I felt it—that tension in the air, like something was being arranged behind my back.

And in Puerto Rico, back then, men married girls my age all the time. It wasn't even hidden. It was whispered about in kitchens, in church pews, in family circles. Thirteen. Fourteen. Sometimes, even younger. Girls being handed off like property under the guise of religion and tradition.

So I started to wonder: Was that what she was doing with me?

Was I being groomed? Offered? Promised?

The same dread I thought I'd escaped came rushing back. I didn't feel safe anymore. I felt watched. I felt planned. And once again, I found myself alone in a place that told me I should be grateful just to exist.

And I didn't know it yet, but that's exactly what she was grooming me for. I was supposed to be his child bride. Not just a visitor. Not just someone being watched over. A bride. A possession. A body to be handed over like it was part of some unspoken agreement. I didn't fully understand it at the time, but I could feel it. The way he looked at me. The way she spoke around me, not to me, as if my life was something she could negotiate. In exchange, she got money. Quietly. Discreetly. Enough to keep her satisfied. She got a brand-new TV. I remember it arriving, still wrapped in plastic, the remote taped to the top. She beamed at it like it was a trophy like it meant she'd done something right. And I got nothing but fear. A fear that didn't sleep. A fear that clung to my skin like sweat. I'd lie awake at night imagining myself trapped in that man's house, being forced to smile, to serve, to survive all over again. I knew I had to get out. There was no option. No hesitation. My body screamed it. My heart knew it before my mind did.

So, the next time the social worker came, I lost it. I didn't hold back. I made noise. I made chaos. I shattered the silence that had always protected the adults around me. I caused such a scene that they had no choice. They couldn't ignore me this time. I made sure of it. They called Anna. I was going back to Florida. The irony didn't escape me that I was being sent back to the very place I once escaped. But in that moment, even that seemed safer than being sold.

Sylvia kept me for a few days until the plane tickets were bought. She didn't speak much. I didn't either. I kept my head down, kept my guard up, kept my hope just barely alive. I didn't unpack. I didn't exhale. I just waited, praying silently that the plane would come before anything else did.

I just wanted to disappear. I wandered the streets as night fell, searching for somewhere safe to sleep. I found a small spot behind a store, grabbed a piece of cardboard, and laid it down like a bed. I pretended I was back in Florida, hiding in the woods with Luis. Then I closed my eyes.

The next morning, I woke up to police officers standing over me. They asked for my name. I told them. And just like that, I was taken back to Sylvia. I thought that meant my time in Puerto Rico was over. But it wasn't. Sylvia called HRS again. This time, they took me away for good. I was placed in a new foster home. The woman was a religious fanatic, strict, controlling. Church five times a week. No TV. No playtime. Just prayer.

At first, I thought, Okay, at least it's not like before. Then I noticed something. She kept taking me to her neighbor's house, a truck driver, a grown man. In Puerto Rico, back then, men married girls my age all the time.

And I didn't know it yet, but that's exactly what she was grooming me for. I was supposed to be his child bride. In exchange, she got money.

She got a brand-new TV. And I got nothing but fear. I knew I had to get out. So, the next time the social worker came, I lost it. I caused such a scene that they had no choice. They called Anna. I was going back to Florida. Sylvia kept me for a few days until the plane tickets were bought.

Luis and I packed up what little we had. A few worn-out clothes, a pair of shoes, and a toothbrush with bent bristles. It wasn't much, but it was ours. And just like that, we were going back home. Or rather, back to Anna's house because it never really felt like home. Home is where you're wanted. Where you're safe. Anna's house was neither. But it was familiar, and in a strange, twisted way, that familiarity was almost comforting. Almost.

The happiness of leaving Puerto Rico was short-lived. There was no celebration. No sigh of relief. Just a quiet ride to the airport, a plane ticket that felt like a lifeline, and a heart weighed down with dread. Because I already knew what was waiting for us there. The yelling. The rules. The silence. The way she looked at us like we were burdens, not blessings.

And when we landed and saw Anna's face, I braced myself. Her expression was unreadable—tight-lipped, arms crossed, jaw set. Not a hug. Not a smile. Just that cold stare that said everything without saying a word. I swallowed hard, my fingers tightening around the strap of my bag. Luis stayed close to my side. We didn't speak. We didn't need to. We had done this before.

I braced myself. For the coldness. As a punishment. For the disappointment she'd carry in her voice. I braced myself for the reminder that we were not loved. That we were back under her roof but not under her care.

I braced myself.

For whatever hell was about to come next.

CHAPTER 8
THE NEW LISA

Fights became a regular thing for me. I was always ready to swing, always ready to defend myself because if I didn't, who would? No one ever stood up for me. No one ever stepped in. I learned early that if I didn't fight for myself, I'd be eaten alive. So I kept my fists ready, my eyes hard, my back straight, even when I was exhausted, even when all I really wanted was to be left alone.

The girls in the detention center made sure I never forgot that I was different. They called me a white girl because of the way I talked—too proper, too clean, too "other" for them. It didn't matter that I came from the same pain, the same struggle, the same streets. To them, I was soft. Or at least, I looked at it. And that made me a target.

They mocked my long, curly hair—the way it frizzed in humidity, the way it fell into my eyes. My mixed-race features confused them and irritated them. They didn't know what to make of me, and so they made me a joke. A punching bag. A mirror they didn't like looking into. Sometimes, they would sit behind me and twist my curls between their fingers, acting like it was a game.

And then they'd yank it. Hard. Laughing like it was funny like it didn't sting, like it didn't make me want to disappear all over again.

But I didn't disappear. I turned around. And I swung. Because I had no other choice.

Some days, they'd put things in my hair—gum, pieces of food, whatever they could find—just to humiliate me. They'd wait until I wasn't looking, or they'd do it right in front of me, laughing as they pressed something sticky or rotten into my curls like it was all just a game. I'd feel the tug, the wetness, the crunch, and know immediately something was wrong. They didn't care how it made me feel. They wanted a reaction. They wanted to see me squirm, to remind me that I didn't belong, that I was easy to target, easy to break.

And the names Ugly. Skinny. Disgusting. Nobody wants you. That's why you don't have a mother. You're nothing. They didn't just say the words—they spat them, made sure I heard them loud and clear and made sure I absorbed them. They followed me down the hallway, whispered them while I ate, and chanted them under their breath when I walked by like a curse being cast again and again.

It was relentless. Every day, every hour, another reminder that I didn't matter, that I was less than them. Most days, I believed them. It was easier to believe them than to fight back. Maybe they were right. Maybe I was nothing. Maybe I really was ugly, skinny, disgusting, unwanted. I looked in the mirror and didn't see myself anymore—I saw their words reflected back at me.

I stopped brushing my hair. I stopped looking people in the eye. I shrank inside my own body, trying to disappear from a world that had already decided I didn't belong in it. That was when my low self-esteem started to take root, and once it did, it never really let go. It grew quietly, wrapping itself around my thoughts, my confidence, and my sense of worth. It whispered to me even when they weren't around. It convinced me I didn't deserve better.

And even as I got older, those same words stayed with me, lingering in the back of my mind like old bruises that never fully faded.

Even now, I still feel it clinging to me, whispering those same words in the back of my mind. No matter how much time passes, no matter how much healing I try to do, the damage remains. There were nights I would pray: God, take this away from me. Make me feel like I look. Make me see what other people see. But that prayer was never answered. I still didn't see it. I still don't.

And those girls? They weren't just cruel with their words. Some of them used me, too. I had already been through enough in my life to understand what it meant to be taken advantage of, to be used for someone else's pleasure, and in the detention center, it happened again.

Except this time, it was with a girl. My first encounter with a woman. It wasn't planned. It wasn't something I'd thought about. It just happened quietly, in the dark, when the world was asleep, and no one was watching. I didn't fight it, didn't resist, because by then, I had already accepted the idea that love—any kind of love—came with a price. That nothing came for free. That affection always had a cost.

I had been taught that if someone wanted you, it usually meant they wanted something from you. And if giving them that meant I wouldn't feel alone, even for a moment, then I gave it. Willingly. Numbly. Like it was just another transaction in a life filled with silent exchanges. And if that's what I had to do to feel something, to feel wanted, then so be it.

I wasn't searching for sex. I wasn't exploring. I wasn't curious. I was desperate. Desperate to feel seen. Desperate to feel held. Desperate to feel like I belonged to someone, somewhere, even if just for a few minutes. At that point, I didn't care who it was. Man, woman, stranger—it didn't matter. I had long stopped believing in the fantasy of being loved without conditions. I just wanted someone to love me. Or pretend to. Pretend hard enough that I could believe it, even if only for the night. Because that fleeting feeling, that whisper of closeness, was better than the cold emptiness that lived inside me.

But not everyone in that place was cruel. There were moments—tiny moments—where kindness slipped through the cracks. A shared snack. A word of encouragement. A stolen laugh between tears. Little things that reminded me I was still human and that not everyone was there to break me. And sometimes, that was enough to keep me going. Just knowing someone didn't hate me was enough to survive another day.

I went to the detention center so many times that it almost felt like a second home. The walls, the sounds, the routines—they all became familiar. The clank of doors, the hum of fluorescent lights, the smell of overcooked food and cheap cleaning supplies—it was a rhythm I came to know too well.

Most of the staff rotated in and out, faces blurring together, people who barely looked at you unless you were causing a problem. But that's where I met Amanda.

Amanda was different. She was strong, kind, and beautiful. A Black woman who carried herself with a quiet grace that I admired. She didn't need to raise her voice to be respected. There was something in her presence—solid, calm, unshakable—that made even the toughest girls listen. She didn't walk like she was above us; she walked like she understood us. Like maybe she had once been one of us.

If I could have chosen my mother, she would have looked like Amanda. She had the kind of beauty that wasn't just skin-deep. It radiated from her spirit, from the way she spoke to people, from the care she took in the smallest things.

When I was a little girl, I used to dream that my real mother looked just like her. I imagined a woman who would brush my hair, who would tell me I was special, who would fight for me. And Amanda, in some strange and healing way, stepped into that role. She treated me like a daughter. She saw me not as some lost, angry, broken kid but as a person. As someone worthy of attention, of kindness, of softness.

She asked how I was really doing and waited for the answer. She remembered my favorite snack. She knew when I needed space and when

I needed to be pulled close. And I think, in her own way, she truly loved me. Not because she had to, not because it was part of her job, but because she saw something in me worth loving.

But I was so damaged, so torn apart by everything I had been through, that I didn't know how to accept it. I didn't know how to believe it was real. I kept waiting for her to disappear, to turn cold, to betray me like everyone else had.

Love felt like a foreign language, something I could hear but never quite understand. I could feel it brushing against me, trying to wrap itself around my bruised heart, but I didn't know how to open the door to let it in. So I held it at arm's length, aching for it and fearing it all at once.

Every time someone had claimed to care for me, it came with conditions, with pain. Love always seemed to wear a mask, a disguise that would eventually fall away to reveal something darker underneath. There were always strings attached: be good, be quiet, be useful, be available. Love meant sacrifice. Love meant giving something up. Love meant losing a piece of myself just to feel seen for a moment. I didn't know how to trust real love, so I kept my guard up. I built walls so high no one could climb them, not even the ones who meant well. I questioned every kind word, braced for the moment when the smile would disappear, and the hand would strike, or the voice would change. Even when Amanda looked at me with softness in her eyes, I found it hard to look back. I was afraid to hope. Afraid to believe That may be this time, but it was different. I didn't know how to let

Amanda in. Not because I didn't want to but because I didn't know how. My heart had been hardened by too many broken promises, too many nights crying in silence, too many people walking away. Amanda tried. I saw her trying. But I had learned that getting close meant getting hurt. So, I stayed distant. I laughed at the wrong times. I changed the subject. I pushed back.

The Cycle Continues Life after the detention center became a revolving door. I would get out, but I had nowhere to go, so I would get caught up in the same things: running away, stealing to survive, finding shelter wherever I could. It wasn't because I wanted to live that way; it was because I had no choice. The world didn't offer me options, only consequences. There was no welcome home, no bed waiting, no open arms. Just the streets, the cold, and the hunger. And before I knew it, I'd be back inside. It was almost like I belonged there more than I belonged anywhere else. I hated that truth, but I couldn't escape it. On the outside, I had no stability, no home, no real sense of safety. Every night was a gamble. I was either sleeping in abandoned houses with floors that smelled of mildew and rot, running from the past that haunted me, or doing whatever I had to do to survive. That meant lying, stealing, hiding, and trusting the wrong people just to make it to the next day.

But inside the detention center? There was a routine. There were rules and structure. Even if it was a place meant to punish, for me, it was almost a relief. At least in there, I knew what to expect. I knew when I'd eat. I knew when the lights would go out. I knew no one could walk in and hurt me in the middle of the night. It was twisted, but it felt like safety. Not freedom but safety. And that's something I rarely had. But the more time I spent locked away, the angrier I became. The walls that once gave me structure started to feel like they were closing in. The routine that gave me peace began to feel like a cage. I was tired of being a victim, tired of people seeing me as weak. I was tired of being pitied, tired of being underestimated, tired of being the broken girl everyone passed over.

I started changing, toughening up, and becoming someone I thought I needed to be. I looked in the mirror and stopped seeing a child. I saw a survivor, a fighter. I told myself that the only way to survive was to become hard, to become dangerous, to stop caring about anything or anyone. I couldn't afford to feel anymore. Feelings got you hurt. Feelings got you killed. And that's exactly what I did. I shut everything down. I stopped crying. I stopped dreaming. I stopped hoping. I started fighting back more, not just reacting but throwing the first punch. I didn't wait to be cornered. I struck first. I made sure no one could say I was weak again. I became the very thing the world had taught me to be: ruthless. And in that anger, in that armor, I finally felt powerful. But deep down, I didn't realize I was just building a different kind of cage—one made of rage instead of walls.

If someone so much as looked at me wrong, I was ready to swing. My body stayed tense, coiled like a spring, waiting for the smallest excuse to explode. I had learned the hard way that hesitation could cost you. That looking soft got you hurt. So I met every glare with a stare twice as hard.

I refused to let anyone make me feel small again. I'd been belittled, laughed at, discarded, used, and I swore to myself it would never happen again. If I were going to be known for something, I'd rather be feared than pitied. Pity made people uncomfortable. Fear made them stay back. I figured that if no one could love me, at least they'd learn not to mess with me.

I stopped crying myself to sleep. Tears felt like a weakness I couldn't afford anymore. I stopped wishing for love. It didn't seem like something meant for people like me. Love was a fairy tale that always ended in disappointment. I stopped believing in happy endings. I started to see them as lies we tell ourselves to get through the day. The new Lisa was forming, and she was nothing like the girl I used to be. She didn't need comfort. She didn't need anyone. She built walls around her heart so high that even she couldn't climb over them anymore.

But in the middle of all that change, there was Amanda.

Amanda's Impact Even as I hardened myself to the world, Amanda never gave up on me. She didn't flinch when I raised my voice. She didn't walk away when I tried to push her. She stood her ground, patient and steady, like she knew what I was doing and loved me anyway. She saw something in me, something no one else had ever bothered to see. Not just potential but worth. She looked past the rage, the sharp tongue, the cold eyes. She saw the girl underneath—the scared, aching, hurting girl who still wanted to be held.

And even when I pretended not to care, even when I rolled my eyes or shut down, her presence stayed. She was a light I didn't know I needed. And deep down, that mattered more than I could ever admit out loud.

She talked to me like I was more than just a troubled girl with a messed-up past like I was someone worth saving. Her voice was calm, never pitying, never forceful. Just steady, like a soft drumbeat in the background of my chaos.

"Lisa," she would say, "You don't have to let this life turn you into something you're not."

Her words lingered in the air long after she walked away, like incense that clung to the walls of my thoughts. But I didn't believe her. Not then. Not when everything I had been through told me otherwise. I had already let the world shape me. I had already become someone else. Someone hard. Someone angry. Someone who didn't cry anymore. Someone who struck first and never looked back.

I didn't know how to go back to whoever I used to be before the pain started carving me into pieces. Still, she tried. Day after day, conversation after conversation, Amanda didn't give up. She didn't treat me like a project. She didn't treat me like a burden. She treated me like I mattered like I wasn't just a number in the system. Like I wasn't broken beyond repair. She remembered things about me—small things that no one else ever noticed. My favorite snack. The way I tensed when someone walked too close. The nights I didn't sleep.

And in those rare moments when I let my guard down when I stopped fighting for just a second, I could feel something deep inside me wanting to believe her, wanting to believe that maybe, just maybe, I wasn't too far gone. That there was still some light left in me. That I was more than what I'd been through.

But I was scared to trust myself. Scared that if I started to hope, I would be let down all over again. Scared that if I believed in healing, I'd only end up hurt. So I held back. I smiled with my lips but not with my heart. I nodded but didn't commit. Because trusting her meant believing I deserved more, and I wasn't ready to believe that yet.

Every time I had trusted someone before, they had let me down. They said they cared, then disappeared. They promised safety, then turned on me. They smiled with kindness, then used me. So, no matter how much Amanda tried to reach me, there was always a wall between us—a wall I had built brick by brick, with every betrayal, every slap, every night I cried alone. I wish I could say that my time with Amanda changed me instantly, that I saw the light and turned my life around. I wish I could say she saved me that her words cracked open my heart, and all the pain poured out, and everything got better. But that's not how life works, especially when you've been through as much as I had. Healing doesn't come like a lightning bolt—it's more like a flicker in the dark, a barely-there warmth you're too numb to notice at first. When I left the detention center, I was still lost. Still dragging my past like a heavy bag tied to my ankle. I was still angry. Still full of fire and fight and the need to protect myself at all costs.

I was still the new Lisa—the one who didn't take shit from anyone, who wasn't afraid to hurt before being hurt, who had learned that love came at a cost, and who had already paid it too many times to believe it was ever worth it.

But Amanda planted something in me. A seed. A small, quiet thing that didn't grow right away. A tiny whisper of hope that maybe one day, I would be more than what life had made me. More than just the broken girl who survived. More than the fists, the silence, the scars. I just wasn't ready to listen yet. I wasn't ready to let that seed grow. I kept it buried, deep beneath the anger, beneath the pain, beneath the armor I had worn for so long; it felt like skin.

At this point, I was still in the detention center, trying to adjust to life there—to the routines, the people, the silence that screamed louder at night. I was doing what I always did: survive. Then someone told me something that made my heart stop: Luis was there too. Those words hit me like a punch to the chest. Luis. My baby brother. My other half. The one person in this world who had ever truly seen me needed me and loved me. And now he was here too, locked away, caught in the same cycle, walking the same path. My chest tightened with guilt, with fear, with rage. What had they done to him? What had life done to him? I thought I had failed him. I thought I had lost him. But deep down, something else stirred—something stronger than anger. It was love. Fierce, desperate, protective love. And at that moment, I knew I had to find him. I had to see him. I had to hold him and remind him that no matter what, we were still in this together.

I couldn't believe it. My little brother? Here? In this place? It didn't feel real. My chest tightened as the words sank in, and I could feel my hands shaking with a mix of panic, disbelief, and an aching kind of sadness I couldn't put into words. I had to find him. I didn't care what it took. I needed to see his face, to know he was okay, to remind myself that he was still here, still breathing, still mine.

I searched every hallway with my heart pounding in my ears. And when I did find him, the moment was bittersweet. There he was—Luis. My Luis. He looked at me with those same big, innocent eyes—eyes that had seen too much but still held that childlike softness that made me want to wrap him up and never let go. And he said, "Lisa, I stole a car. I couldn't be by myself for Christmas. I knew you were going to be in here." That broke me. His voice was calm, like it made perfect sense like it was the most natural thing in the world to do something so wild just to be near me. That was the kind of bond we had. Even in his pain, in his loneliness, his first thought was to find me. To be with me. He needed me. And I needed him just as much.

Even though Luis was my brother, he felt more like my son. I had raised him in a hundred small ways—feeding him, dressing him, wiping his tears when no one else would. I carried his burdens like they were my own because they were. My best friend. My everything. The one person who never gave up on me, never looked at me like I was too much or not enough. We were only a year apart, but I had always seen myself as his protector. I was his safe place, and he was mine. He was all I had, and I was all he had. And knowing that this world had swallowed him up the same way it had swallowed me—it shattered something inside me that had already been cracked too many times to count. But seeing him there, breathing the same air, wearing the same uniform, looking at me like I was still his hero—I knew I couldn't fall apart. Not yet. Not in front of him. I had to stay strong, even if it was just for a moment. Because if I fell, we'd both fall. And I couldn't let that happen. Not to him. Not ever.

No matter where we ended up, no matter what the hell we were thrown into, we always found our way back to each other. Like magnets drawn together by pain, by love, by survival—we always somehow circled back. The world tried to separate us, to break us apart piece by piece, but it never worked. We clung to each other like lifelines, like our souls knew that one couldn't breathe without the other. That Christmas, we spent it together, locked up in the detention center. It was cold, quiet, stripped of joy and lights and music. But none of that mattered. We had each other. Just the two of us, sitting in that grey-walled place, finding warmth in a look, in shared memory, in knowing we weren't alone. We didn't need presents. We didn't need decorations. All we needed was that one truth: we were still together.

And even now, after all this time, to this day, I am haunted by the regret of Luis following me to the detention center. It eats at me. I replay it in my mind like a film I can't turn off, wondering how it might've been different if I had made better choices. If I had shielded him harder, loved him louder, and protected him more. I regret allowing him to do whatever it took to stay by my side. He shouldn't have had to do that. He shouldn't have had to break the laws or risk everything just to feel close to me. I was supposed to lead him somewhere better, and instead, I led him straight into the same fire I was trying to crawl out of. Luis has his own story, his own troubles, and his own testimony, but this is one of my deepest regrets. The kind that never lets go. The kind that sits in your chest like a brick and never moves.

The weight of this regret is something I will carry until the day God takes the life out of my body. It's stitched into me, bone-deep. A shadow that follows me wherever I go. If I could change one thing from my past, it would be to shield Luis from the pain of depending on me, following me, copying me, and just trying to be with me. He didn't know any better. He just wanted to stay close, to not lose me, to survive the only way he knew how—by my side. And I let him. I let him follow me into the darkness. The things he had to endure behind those walls because he wanted to follow his big sister are a burden I can't bear. They haunt me in the quiet moments. When I see kids his age smiling without a care in the world. When I think about what his life could've been without all that pain. The guilt and sorrow are overwhelming, and I struggle to live with it even now. I smile, I breathe, I move through the world, but inside, there's a piece of me that will always be broken by that truth. And nothing I do will ever be enough to make it right.

A New Beginning Not long after, my time at the detention center was coming to an end. My release date was approaching, and with it came a strange mix of emotions: fear, relief, and uncertainty all tangled together. That chapter of my life—the fights, the torment, the constant battles— was closing. I had spent so long inside those walls that I didn't know what freedom really meant anymore. I had been shaped by survival, hardened by pain, and I didn't know if the world outside could hold anything different for me.

But something unexpected happened. Something I never could've imagined. Amanda, the woman who had treated me like a daughter, the woman who saw me for more than just a troubled, broken girl, wanted me to come live with her. I didn't believe it at first. I thought maybe I had misunderstood. People like her didn't take in girls like me. Girls with records. Girls with trust issues and anger, and years of trauma.

But she meant it. She wanted me, not out of pity. Not to fix me. But because she genuinely cared. Because somewhere along the way, she saw something in me that was worth saving.

For a moment, hope flickered inside me. It was soft, hesitant, but real. That little glow in the center of my chest that I hadn't felt in so long. Maybe, just maybe, this was my chance. A real home. A clean slate. A place where I wouldn't have to fight every second just to exist. A place where someone wanted me not for what I could offer but simply for who I was.

I was scared to believe in it, scared to hold onto it too tightly, in case it disappeared like everything else in my life. But something in me wanted to try. To lean in. To see what could happen if, for once, I said yes to love instead of running from it. Amanda was offering me a lifeline. And for the first time in a long time, I was ready to reach for it.

But there was a catch. Before I could go live with Amanda, I had to complete six months at Eckerd Wilderness Camp. It felt like one more obstacle placed in front of me, one more test to pass before I could finally breathe. Part of me was disappointed. I was so close to something that resembled a real home, and now I had to wait again. But I knew I didn't have a choice. If this was the road I had to take to get to Amanda, then I was going to walk it.

I attended Eckerd Wilderness Camp, specifically the Camp E-NINI-HASSE location in Floral City, Florida, around 1993. The name itself felt strange, almost like a code for some secret society I didn't ask to join. This camp was originally established in 1968 as a therapeutic program for boys—a place where the "unruly" or "unfixable" could be sent to be straightened out. It had that old-school energy: tough love, survival tactics, emotional endurance.

In 1969, they expanded to include a program for troubled girls who faced emotional or behavioral challenges. Girls like me. Girls who had been labeled, judged, and written off. These camps were located throughout Florida, tucked away in remote areas surrounded by nature, far from the noise of the cities, far from distractions, and far from any place you could run.

They believed in isolation and immersion, in stripping away all the noise and getting to the root of their pain through hard work, long hikes, and strict discipline. No phones. No music. No contact with the outside world. Just the wilderness, your counselors, and whatever demons you had carried with you.

I didn't know what to expect. I had never been camping before, never slept under the stars unless I was homeless. Now, I was being told this was therapy. This was healing. And I was supposed to find myself in the middle of nowhere.

All I knew was I had to survive it. Because on the other side of this journey, Amanda was waiting. And I wasn't going to lose that chance. Not this time.

My experience was at the E-NINI-HASSE camp, which was designed for troubled youth like myself, girls who had slipped through the cracks, who had been tossed from one system to the next, who were teetering on the edge of something worse. The camp wasn't just a place to send us away—it was a last effort to redirect our paths before we reached the point of no return.

The camp aimed to provide us with a second chance at life and reintegration into society before potentially being sent to more severe level eight or ten programs. And make no mistake, those programs weren't just stricter—they were darker, harder, and filled with girls who had lost almost all hope of returning to a normal life.

For context, these programs are intended for girls who have encountered legal issues, such as detention centers. Girls who had faced judges, courtrooms, probation officers. Girls who, like me, had already seen too much.

Before resorting to such measures, individuals were first sent to an Eckerd Wilderness Camp, which had several locations across Florida at that time. These camps were part of a larger system that tried to catch us before we fell all the way through. They were deep in the woods—far from distractions, far from temptations, and far from the streets we'd come to know too well.

The idea was that nature, structure, and discipline could help reset us, break us down, and build us back up. And for many, it was the last opportunity to prove they could turn things around. I didn't know yet what the wilderness would do to me. I only knew that I didn't want to end up in a level eight or ten facility. I had already seen the inside of enough cold, locked buildings to know that I couldn't go through that again.

If this camp were my chance to rewrite my story, I was willing to try, even if it scared me. Even if I didn't believe I was worth saving just yet. I still had Amanda's offer waiting. And I held onto that like a lifeline.

Regrettably, most of these camps have since been shut down. Between 1985 and 2015, there were numerous allegations of abuse, several fatalities, and a class-action lawsuit filed by parents who had entrusted these camps with their children.

This Is A Photo When I Was With John (My Son, Valentino Ortiz).

This is Luise Ortiz-Acker. This was how some of the prison yards looked.

LOWELL CORRECTIONAL INSTITUTION

These Were The Showers That We Had To Use When We Were In Either The Mental Health Dorm Or Confinement.

This was the average meal for us in the prison.

Here is the image of the Camp E-Nini-Hassee

This camp was originally established in 1968 as a therapeutic program for boys. In 1969, they expanded to include a program for troubled girls who faced emotional or behavioral challenges. These camps were located throughout Florida.

Me and My Daughter Marliesia Ortiz, Around 1999

Here is the picture of my brother, still in prison.

I was released on January 2, 2021, from the Department of Corrections. My son drove to Miami, Florida, on January 5, 2021, to come and see me.

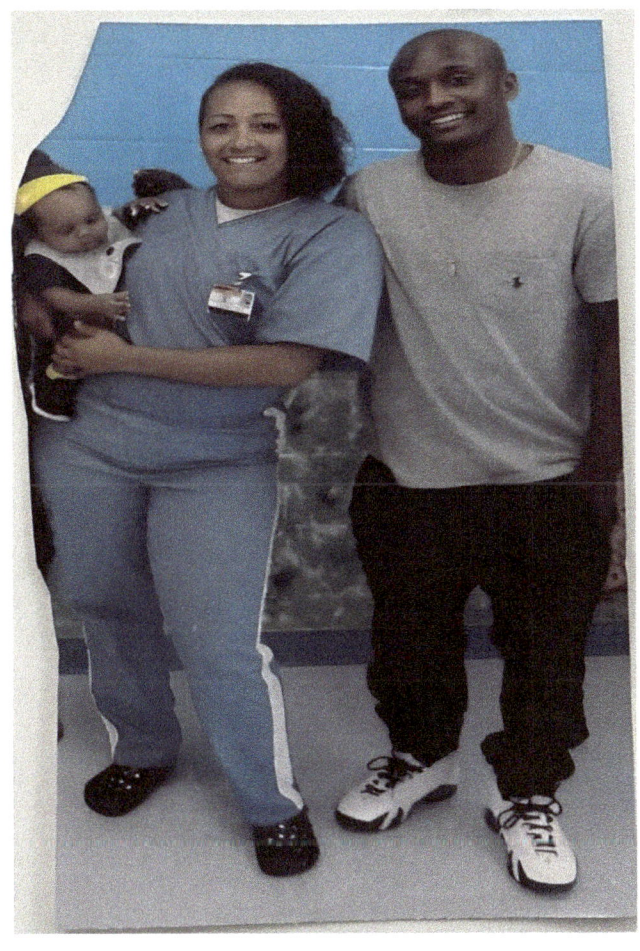

That's Me And My Son At Visitation At Florida Women's
Correctional Institution. He Was Bringing Up My Grandbaby To
See Me.

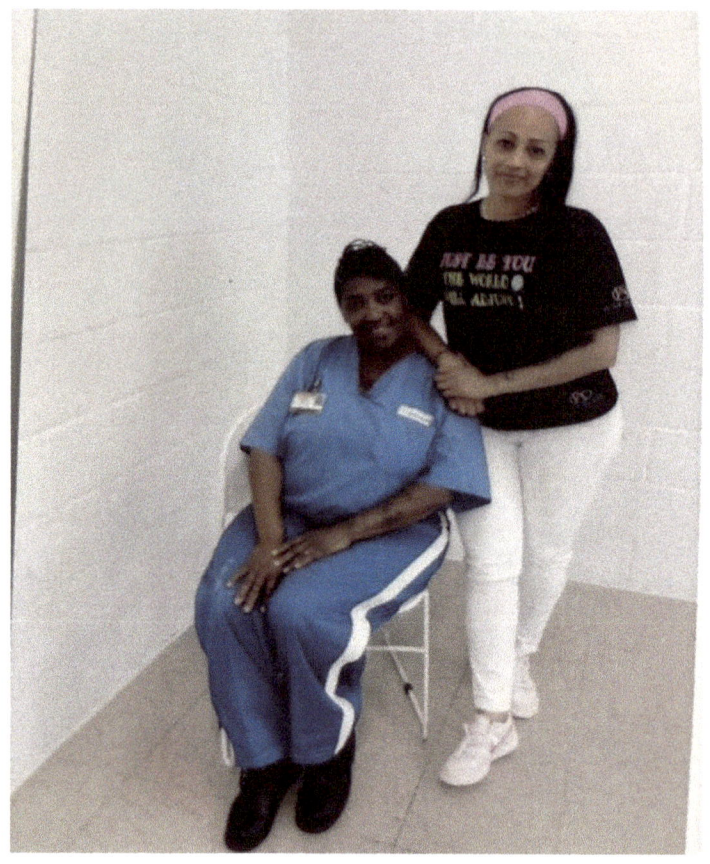

That's me and my friend Patsy Jones. She's currently incarcerated at Holmstead Correctional Institution, doing a natural life sentence for murder. Those are some of the many women that I do prison outreach with.

Me and My Foster Cousin Antoinette

CHAPTER 9:
GLIMPSE OF NORMAL

At this point, I was still staying with Amanda, trying to adjust to what felt like a normal life. The idea of normalcy was foreign to me. I wasn't used to waking up in the same bed every morning, eating meals at a kitchen table, or hearing someone ask how my day was and actually mean it. For the first time in a long time, I had stability: a home, food, clothes, and someone who actually cared about me. Amanda made sure I never felt like a burden. She gave me space when I needed it and guidance when I was spiraling. But deep inside, I was still lost. I had spent so many years in survival mode that peace felt uncomfortable—almost like I didn't deserve it. I didn't know how to sit still without waiting for the next storm.

Between 1992 and early 1993, Amanda enrolled me in De Soto High School in Arcadia, Florida, where I started ninth grade. The school was big, filled with new faces, new routines, and new expectations. Walking those halls felt overwhelming. I didn't make many friends, but I didn't expect to because I've always been a loner. I kept to myself, head down, focused on just getting through the day. Trusting people was still hard. I didn't know who was genuine and who would turn on me the moment I let my guard down.

However, that didn't stop some girls from trying to bully me. They saw my silence as weakness, my loner nature as an invitation to push buttons. Some whispered things as I walked by. Others tested me with looks, trying to provoke a reaction. But I had been through worse. I had survived worse. I knew how to hold my own. As a tomboy, I ran track and even tried out for the high school football team. I needed an outlet—something to pour my energy and anger into. Sports gave me that. Running made me feel free like I was outrunning my past.

Football was a different beast. Training with the boys was incredibly tough and painful. Every hit, every sprint, every bruise reminded me that I was still fighting—not just for a place on the team, but for a place in the world. I didn't want to be seen as fragile. I wanted them to know I could take the hits and keep going. Because that's what I'd been doing my whole life.

I have to say, being part of that team was hard work. The training was brutal. The drills were intense. Every day left my muscles sore, my body aching, and my mind drained. I pushed myself past the point of exhaustion, sweating through practices that felt like they were designed to break people. And sometimes, I think they were. But I kept showing up. Kept grinding. Kept pushing through the pain because giving up just wasn't in me.

Did I make it all the way? No, of course not. I didn't end up on the final roster and didn't run out onto the field in a helmet and pads on game day. But I didn't see that as a failure. I saw it as something more important—a stand. Not because I expected to, but because I was a girl. Not in that space. Not at that time. The odds were stacked from the moment I stepped onto the field. But I knew that walking in. I wasn't naïve. I wasn't chasing glory. I was chasing equality.

Honestly, I only did it because I felt the school didn't want me to because of my gender. There was something in the way the coaches looked at me, the way some of the boys smirked, that made it clear I wasn't supposed to be there. I wasn't welcome. But that only made me want it more. I wanted to prove a point—that girls could do what guys do. That we were just as strong, just as fast, just as determined. I had been fighting my whole life not just for survival but for space. For the right to exist where I wasn't expected to.

So, even though I knew I wouldn't make the final team, I still gave it my all. Every sprint, every hit, every drop of sweat was my way of saying I belong. I may not have left with a jersey, but I walked away with something more powerful: my pride. I showed up in a place where I wasn't wanted, and I didn't back down. And that meant everything.

Around that time, I got really close to Amanda's dad, Frank Walker, whom I used to call Grandpa. There was something about him that instantly felt safe, steady, familiar in a way I didn't know I needed. He didn't treat me like a case or a troubled kid. He treated me like a granddaughter. Like family.

He was mostly confined to a wheelchair due to a bone disease he developed while on the police force. His body had slowed down, but his spirit hadn't. You could still see the fire in his eyes, the sharpness in his mind, and the strength in the way he carried himself—even from that chair. Despite his condition, he became a significant figure in my life. He had a quiet way of teaching, of guiding, without ever making me feel like I was being lectured. Just by being around him, I picked up lessons in patience, resilience, and what it meant to keep showing up even when life tried to knock you down.

He would send me to the store to buy his cigarettes, and somehow, those small errands made me feel trusted and responsible—like I had a role in something. He didn't hover or question me. He'd just give me the money and the brand, and I'd go. It wasn't about the cigarettes—it was about the bond. Those tiny moments of trust added up.

He'd also attend my football practices, sitting there in his wheelchair with that steady presence, watching me run drills and take hits like he was proud just to be there. And that meant everything to me. Someone was showing up for me. Cheering for me.

Frank also taught me how to fix cars, and I learned a lot from him. I'd sit beside him in the garage, grease on my hands, tools scattered on the ground, and listen as he explained what went where, how to listen to the engine, how to pay attention to the details. He never treated me like I couldn't handle it because I was a girl. He treated me like I was capable. Smart. Worth teaching.

Even though Amanda wasn't my real mom, she and her family taught me a great deal. They gave me glimpses into a life I had never known— one with guidance, structure, respect, and, most of all, consistency. They weren't perfect, but they were present. And that alone changed something in me. For the first time in a long time, I felt like I was part of something. Like maybe, just maybe, I wasn't as alone in this world as I had always believed.

I had two close friends during that time. They were the kind of people who showed up in the middle of the chaos and stuck around when everything else felt uncertain. One of them was Trish, a cool white girl with a beautiful face, blonde hair, and gold teeth. She had that kind of confidence that drew people in. There was something wild and fearless about her like she had already seen too much of the world to be scared of anything.

We met in the detention center and stayed friends for a long time. Every time I went to a program or the detention center, there was Trish. Somehow, no matter where I ended up, we always crossed paths again. It was like the universe kept placing us in each other's lives to remind us we weren't completely alone. She was like a mirror—sometimes flawed, strong, hurting, laughing through the pain. We understood each other without having to explain much. There weren't many people I trusted back then, but Trish was one of them.

My foster cousin Antoinette was my main girl. She wasn't just family by circumstance—she was my sister by heart. We did everything together, from hanging out to getting into trouble. There was never a dull moment with her. We were always plotting, always on the move, always trying to find something to make us feel alive.

Every weekend, we'd go to Walmart, and, like many teenagers, we'd steal things like Polaroid film, clothes, and beads. It wasn't about what we took—it was about the thrill, the rush, the rebellion. We were just two girls trying to take control of a life that so often made us feel powerless. We wanted to look good, feel seen, feel like we mattered in a world that constantly overlooked us. We laughed a lot and got caught a few times, but mostly, we just made memories—some foolish, some painful, but all ours.

Antoinette is still my cousin to this day, and we stay in touch. Through all the changes, all the distance, all the years that tried to pull us apart, she's still there. And there's something comforting about that— knowing that someone who knew the version of me with all the scars and rough edges still chooses to keep me close.

During that period, I also got a job working in the watermelon fields, and that's where I met my first child's father, Eddie Hillman. The work was hard—backbreaking, sweat-dripping, sun-scorching labor. The Florida heat in the middle of summer didn't care that I was just a teenager. The air was thick and heavy, and the ground seemed to radiate heat that baked into your skin. I'd spend hours bending over, lifting heavy watermelons, my hands getting rougher by the day. But I didn't complain.

One thing I've always done is hustle or keep a job. That's just who I am. Even as a kid, I understood that if I wanted anything—clothes, food, respect—I had to get it myself. I never had anything I wanted, so I made sure to work or hustle to keep money in my pocket and take care of myself. No one was handing me anything, and I didn't expect them to. Even though I was in a good space, living with Amanda and trying to stay on the right path, I still wanted to be self-sufficient, and I'm still like that to this day.

Being dependent made me feel vulnerable, and I had already learned what happens when you depend on the wrong people. One of my first jobs was working in the watermelon fields, picking watermelons in the hot, sticky summer. There were a lot of men from Georgia and many older guys who'd been doing that kind of work for years. They were rough, sun-worn, and always had something slick to say.

At that time, I was in ninth grade, still trying to find my footing, still straddling the line between childhood and adulthood. This is where I met Eddie Hillman. He was much older than me and quickly reeled me in. He had that charm, that street smoothness, the kind of confidence that made girls feel chosen. And I was still a child—craving attention and love, starved for validation—so he was able to manipulate me and use me as he wanted.

I didn't see it then. I thought I was in control. I thought I was grown. But I wasn't. I was vulnerable, and he saw that. Eddie taught me how to cook crack because, besides working in the fields, he was also selling drugs on the side. The fieldwork was just a cover. The real money came from the streets. And I was so eager to please him, to feel needed, that I let him pull me in deeper.

He introduced me to the drug game, having me cook and sell crack for him. He showed me how to measure it, how to cut it, how to package it. I was just a kid, but I was playing in a world that could eat grown men alive. And I did it because I thought it made me valuable. I thought it meant I had a place. I didn't realize I was being used until it was too late. By then, I was already in too deep.

Did I have to do all this? No, because at that time, I was staying with Amanda, who was treating me well. She gave me a roof over my head, food in the kitchen, clothes on my back, and something even more important: stability. She didn't just provide the basics; she gave me a sense of safety, something I hadn't felt in years. She was consistent, patient, and genuinely wanted the best for me. I had no reason to be out in the streets. I wasn't desperate for shelter or starving for food. But trauma doesn't always care about logic. My mind was so messed up that I felt it was okay to be doing that. Somewhere deep down, I still didn't believe I deserved the good things Amanda was offering me. I didn't know how to exist in peace because chaos had become my comfort zone. I was used to survival, not stability. The noise, the danger, the thrill — that was what I understood. That's what felt normal.

I felt stuck and didn't want to get out of that situation. It's not that I didn't see the difference between right and wrong — I did. I just didn't think I was worthy of choosing right. I was too young and naïve to realize that I had a good thing going and shouldn't mess it up. I didn't have the maturity or self-worth to step back and ask myself what I really wanted for my future. I let my pain and my past guide me instead. I clung to Eddie, to the streets, to the game, thinking it made me powerful, thinking it made me grow. I didn't realize that I was trading something real for something that would eventually break me.

In the long run, I did. I messed it up. I lost the chance to fully embrace what Amanda had given me. I chose fast money over peace, illusion over reality. And by the time I realized it, the damage had already been done. I had to learn the hard way that sometimes, the people who really love you don't come with flashes or promises — they come with quiet consistency. And I had walked away from that. Not because I didn't care but because I didn't know how to receive it.

Eddie became my first serious relationship while I was still in school, living with Amanda and working in the watermelon fields with my cousin Nette (Antoinette). It started off like most things in my life — fast, messy, and intense. He gave me the kind of attention I thought I needed, the kind that made me feel wanted, important, and seen. At the time, I didn't realize how much of it was manipulation. I was young, vulnerable, and eager to feel loved, and Eddie knew how to take advantage of that. As time went by, I continued seeing Eddie behind Amanda's back because I knew she would never approve of me being with a grown man. She had been trying so hard to help me build a new life, a better path, and I was out there tearing it all down one secret at a time. I was torn between the safety Amanda gave me and the chaos that felt familiar.

Things at school started getting serious — so serious that I brought a gun to school, which I got from Eddie. I didn't think about the weight of that decision. I just thought I needed to protect myself, to show the world that I wasn't someone to mess with. In my mind, the gun made me powerful and untouchable. But it didn't take long for everything to unravel. I got caught with it and was arrested in the schoolyard. I'll never forget the feeling of those cuffs on my wrists, the stares from the other kids, the shame burning in my chest as the officers led me away. Miss Amanda had to pick me up, and that's how I ended up on probation. It broke something between us that day — not just trust but a piece of the bond we had worked so hard to build. I saw the hurt in her eyes, the disappointment that she tried to hide but couldn't.

Even on probation, I would sneak out the window to see Eddie, hang out with Antoinette, and then sneak back in. I thought I was slick, thought I could move in the shadows without anyone noticing. But I got caught every single time because I wasn't very good at it. I've always been a straight shooter, open about everything, and honestly, I wasn't built to lie or hide. I just didn't care anymore. At that time, I thought, "What more can anyone do to me?" I had already been through so much already felt like I had nothing left to lose. I didn't realize that everything could be taken from me one day. That even the small pieces of stability I had could vanish if I wasn't careful.

I got so caught up with Eddie that, while on probation and attending an alternative school, I was sneaking in and out of the house. I was playing with fire, and I knew it. But the need to feel wanted, to chase something real — even if it was toxic — was stronger than reason. Eventually, I decided to go live with Eddie and his mom, Maggie Hillman, in Georgia. It wasn't planned. It wasn't thought out. I just packed my things and left. I didn't tell Amanda I was leaving, and she was hurt and upset with me. She had taken me in and given me a home, and in return, I disappeared without even telling her. She had offered me stability, love, and safety — and I traded it for chaos. But at that time, I was so caught up in my own pain and my need to find something real that I didn't think about the consequences. I didn't think about how much it would hurt her. I didn't think about what I was giving up. I just needed to feel like I belonged somewhere, and Eddie, for all his flaws, made me feel like I did — even if it was an illusion. And so, I left everything behind, chasing a version of love that would only lead me deeper into the storm.

I was also struggling with the fact that Luis — my brother, my best friend — was placed in a different foster home than me. Being separated from him felt like losing a piece of myself. We had been through everything together — every dark night, every beat-down, every moment of silence when the world forgot about us. He was in Fort Myers, and I hated that we weren't together. I hated it so much it kept me up at night. It didn't matter how far I went or how many people were around me — without Luis, I felt alone. Amanda told me why she couldn't take him in. She already had her own two sons, and she simply didn't have the space for the both of us. She had to choose. And she chose me. She did what she could, and I was grateful, but knowing that didn't make it easier. It didn't soften the ache of not having Luis close. It didn't stop the worry from gnawing at me day and night.

Luis was going on his own path, and it wasn't a good one. I could feel it. Even from a distance, I knew he was spiraling. The streets were calling him, just like they called me once. He got in trouble, and at just 15 years old, he was sentenced to six years in prison for Grand Theft Auto. Six years. A child. My baby brother. Locked away like a grown man. It broke me. I remember when I heard the news — I went numb. My heart didn't just hurt; it shattered. All I could think was I should've been there. I should've stopped it. I should've done something. Guilt flooded me, crushing me like a wave I couldn't swim out of. Here I was in Georgia, pregnant and living with Eddie, and my little brother was locked away. What kind of big sister was I?

Everything in my life still felt unstable, like no matter where I turned, the cycle of loss and pain kept repeating itself. I kept trying to find solid ground, and every time I thought I had, it crumbled beneath me. Every choice I made seemed to ripple out and hurt someone I loved. Luis wasn't just another person to me. He was my heart. My history. My reason. And now he was behind bars, and I couldn't reach him. I couldn't save him. And that kind of helplessness stays with you. It haunts you. It builds a permanent ache inside your chest — a reminder that even when you try your hardest, sometimes love still isn't enough to stop someone from falling.

Luis was going on his own path, and it wasn't a good one. I could feel it. Even from a distance, I knew he was spiraling. The streets were calling him just like they called me once. That pull— the one that tells you the only way to survive is to play the game, to run the streets, to toughen up or be swallowed whole — he felt it, too. And I hated it. I hated watching it happen from far away, knowing the signs, seeing the red flags, but feeling powerless to stop them. He got in trouble, and at just 15 years old, he was sentenced to six years in prison for Grand Theft Auto. Six years. A child. My baby brother. Locked away like a grown man. It broke me. There was no warning, no soft landing — just the news hitting me like a punch straight to the chest.

I remember when I heard the news — I went numb. My heart didn't just hurt; it shattered. I sat in silence, staring at the wall, like if I stayed still enough, maybe it would all go away. All I could think was I should've been there. I should've stopped it. I should've done something. Anything. Guilt flooded me, crushing me like a wave I couldn't swim out of. I replayed everything over and over in my head — where did I go wrong, what could I have said, how did I let him slip away? It felt like I had failed him. Like I had abandoned the one person who needed me the most. Here I was in Georgia, pregnant and living with Eddie, and my little brother was locked away. Locked behind steel bars, with his whole life paused, frozen, tainted by a system that doesn't care about children like him. What kind of big sister was I?

Everything in my life still felt unstable, like no matter where I turned, the cycle of loss and pain kept repeating itself. I couldn't catch a break. I kept chasing peace and kept finding pieces — pieces of hope, pieces of love, pieces of safety — but never the whole thing. I kept trying to find solid ground, and every time I thought I had, it crumbled beneath me. It was like walking on glass barefoot, trying to pretend it didn't hurt. Every choice I made seemed to ripple out and hurt someone I loved. No matter how good my intentions were, it always ended in pain. Luis wasn't just another person to me. He was my heart. My history. My reason. My anchor in the worst of storms. He was the one person who had always been there, who had always loved me through the brokenness, who never judged me. And now he was behind bars, and I couldn't reach him. I couldn't save him. I couldn't take his place. And that kind of helplessness stays with you. It haunts you. It becomes part of your breath, part of your steps, part of your reflection in the mirror. It builds a permanent ache inside your chest — a reminder that even when you try your hardest, even when your love is deep and real, sometimes love still isn't enough to stop someone from falling. And that's a truth I still struggle to live with.

Reality Hits Hard

Being with Eddie wasn't the fairytale I had imagined. At first, it felt like the kind of love I had been waiting for: attention, excitement, a sense of belonging. But beneath all of that was control, manipulation, and pain. I was still young, still naïve, and I didn't truly grasp what a healthy relationship was supposed to look like. I didn't know that love wasn't supposed to hurt, that it wasn't supposed to come with fear or silence or shame. The truth was, he had all the power, and I was just a girl trying to hold on to anything that felt like love. I had confused being wanted with being loved, and in doing so, I lost pieces of myself.

I wasn't making the best decisions. I was reckless with my heart and my body. I ignored the red flags, silenced my instincts, and convinced myself that what we had was real. And as a result, my health suffered. My body started giving me warning signs that I had been ignoring for too long. I contracted multiple infections, each one a painful reminder that I was not okay, that I was risking everything for someone who wasn't truly protecting me. And although I was lucky to never contract anything life-threatening, the experience left me feeling even more broken. I was exhausted, physically and emotionally drained. My body was tired of being mistreated. My spirit was tired of pretending. I was carrying a baby and a weight of sadness that was growing heavier by the day.

Eventually, I reached my breaking point. One day, it all became too much. I couldn't take another lie, another moment of pretending to be okay. I couldn't keep sacrificing myself just to feel loved. I knew I needed to leave. I picked up the phone and called Amanda. My hands were shaking, my heart pounding. I didn't know what to expect. I had walked away from her without a word, turned my back on the only person who had shown me unconditional love, and I wasn't sure she'd even pick up. But she did. She answered. And when she heard my voice, she didn't hesitate. Even though I had left without a word, even though I hurt her, she still welcomed me back with open arms, like her own blood. That's the kind of person Amanda was. She didn't hold grudges. She didn't throw my mistakes in my face. She saw the pain in my voice and opened her heart anyway. No matter how much I tried to push her away, no matter how much I tested her, she never stopped caring about me.

I returned to Florida to Amanda's house, pregnant and lost, but at least I was home. I didn't know what the future held. I didn't know how I was going to raise a child or fix all the things I had broken. But I knew I was safe. I knew I was loved. And for the first time in a long time, I didn't feel like I had to fight just to exist. I was home. And that meant everything.

The Breaking Point

Even though Amanda gave me a second chance, I was still making reckless decisions. I wanted to change. I really did. But wanting something and knowing how to reach it are two very different things. The pain I had buried for years kept surfacing in ways I didn't understand, and instead of facing it, I kept trying to outrun it. I was still breaking the law, still running from my past instead of facing it. Every time I looked in the mirror, I saw someone I didn't recognize—someone hardened, angry, closed off. But underneath all of that, I was still that little girl, scared and lost, just trying to survive. I didn't know how to ask for help without feeling weak. I didn't know how to open up without fearing rejection.

Then, it all caught up to me. Life has a way of doing that—forcing you to stop when you've been running too long. One day, I got caught with a gun at school. It wasn't the first time I had carried one, but this time, I couldn't talk my way out of it. I convinced myself I needed it for protection, that the world was out to hurt me, and I had to be ready. I had been through so much already—abuse, abandonment, betrayal. Carrying a weapon felt like control, like power, like maybe I could finally stop bad things from happening to me. But in reality, I was just a scared, traumatized girl who didn't know how to feel safe. I was carrying years of pain and fear, and it came out in the form of violence, of bad choices, of walls I had built so high no one could climb them—even the people trying to love me.

That mistake cost me everything. In a split second, I lost the trust Amanda had worked so hard to rebuild. I lost my place in school. I lost the fragile grip I had on stability. And most of all, I lost faith in myself. I thought I was making progress, thought I was pulling myself out of the hole I had been trapped in for so long. But one moment of fear-fueled decision-making reminded me just how far I still had to go. And it hurt. It hurt to see the disappointment in Amanda's eyes. It hurt to know that I had once again let down the one person who never gave up on me. It hurt to realize that no matter how badly I wanted to change, I hadn't yet learned how.

A Mother Behind Bars

It was around 1994 when I finally went to jail for my violation of probation after going to Georgia with Eddie. It was like all the consequences I had been outrunning finally caught up with me, surrounding me like a storm I could no longer avoid. I thought I had time to figure things out, thought I could clean things up before anyone noticed.

But life doesn't give you that kind of grace when you've made as many mistakes as I had. When I returned to Amanda's house, thinking maybe I could pick up where I left off, I found out I had a warrant for my arrest. It felt like my whole world stopped at that moment like I couldn't breathe, like the walls were closing in.

I knew I had messed up, but hearing the words "warrant" made everything real in a way I wasn't ready for.

The first thing I saw when I walked in was Trish, my beautiful blonde friend with blue eyes. She had always had this light to her, this charm that made people gravitate toward her. But this time, she wasn't the Trish I knew. Her teeth were rotten, her cheeks sunken in, and she weighed about 90 pounds if that. Her arms were thin and bruised, her skin dull. She had contracted HIV. My heart sank. Trish started off snorting coke, but when that didn't get her high anymore, she turned to crack cocaine. She dove headfirst into the life that so many of us flirted with, believing we could play the game without getting played. She gave her body and soul to the streets, piece by piece until there was nothing left of the girl I used to laugh with, cry with, survive with. Trish was no more. She was a shell of who she used to be, and it broke me. It was like looking into a mirror that showed me who I could become if I didn't change something fast.

I was in the county jail for a little while, and my stomach started swelling just a little bit more as the days went by. I knew what it meant. Life was growing inside me, even as my own life was falling apart. I finally got sentenced to 18 months in the Department of Corrections. That number didn't feel real. A year and a half. Almost two years of my life were taken away before I had even learned how to live. I was also tried as an adult and sent to prison at 17. That title alone—adult—felt like a cruel joke. I was still a child inside, still figuring out who I was, still trying to heal from the wounds that had been left open for years. But the court didn't care. The world didn't care. I was just another statistic, another case file with a birthdate and a charge.

When I arrived at the Department of Corrections, specifically Lowell Correctional Institution, I was young. Scared. Lost. I had only been to the detention center and a couple of youth programs, so I really didn't know what was in store for me when I went to prison. The structure was colder, the stares were harder, the silence heavier. Housed with older inmates, it was a new experience for me. These women had been through things I couldn't yet comprehend, carried stories I wasn't ready to hear, and held pain that echoed my own but in different voices. I was forced to grow up quickly, to learn the rules of survival all over again in an environment that showed no mercy. Every day felt like walking a tightrope—one wrong step and everything could collapse. But I was used to tightropes. I had been walking them my whole life. And now, I would have to walk another one with a child growing inside me and a past that refused to let go.

Even though I was pregnant, I got into many fights because being small, pregnant, and biracial made me an easy target for people in prison who thought they could bully me. They saw someone young, vulnerable, someone who looked like she didn't belong. But that wasn't the case with me. I had already lived through too much, survived too many battles, and earned my stripes long before I ever set foot behind those prison gates. I wasn't about to let anyone walk over me. My size didn't matter—my heart was fierce, and my spirit was sharp. I stood my ground every single time. I wasn't proud of the fights, but they were necessary. They were how I protected myself in a place that showed no mercy.

I was in and out of confinement. It became a cycle—an exhausting, dehumanizing routine that chipped away at me, mentally and physically. This one particular time, I went to an area they called the dungeon. That name wasn't an exaggeration. It was dark, cold, isolated, and it felt like time had stopped back there. You could scream, cry, bang on the walls, and no one would come. The silence was louder than any noise, and it pressed on you until you felt like you were losing your mind. This confinement area is closed now because of what I'm about to tell you.

There was this girl back there with me; she was maybe 16 or 17 years old, around the same age as I was, and she always cried wolf. She'd scream that she was going to kill herself, yell out threats to hurt herself and cry out in desperation over and over again. She was loud, erratic, and clearly in pain, but no one took her seriously. Not the guards. Not the officers.

They just saw her as another "problem inmate," someone they could ignore until shift change. She always said she was going to kill herself, that she was going to do this or that. We were so used to hearing her that even we, the other inmates, started to tune her out. But one day, she cried wolf again—and this time, it wasn't a bluff. She hung herself.

The officers never went back there. They didn't care. They ignored her screams, her threats, her mental breakdowns. She was just another number to them, not a person. And when they finally did their security check, casually, like it was just another routine walkthrough, they found her dead, hanging on the bars. Lifeless. Still. Gone. That image still lives in the back of my mind. It's one of those moments you never forget. The air in that hallway felt colder after that. The silence heavier. I couldn't sleep for days.

I don't even remember her name, but I remember she was a little white girl with black hair, hard eyes, and a troubled soul. She had the kind of pain in her eyes that you don't forget. You could see that she had been through something—that she carried more than any child ever should. I still think about that moment because it showed me that the State, the Department of Corrections, and those officers really didn't care. Not about her. Not about any of us. If they had, they would have taken into account that she was a child and helped her before it became too late. She needed more than a cell. She needed someone to listen, someone to care, someone to see her as a human being. But in that place, humanity was stripped away. And when she died, it wasn't just a tragedy—it was proof. Proof that in that system, young girls like us were disposable. And it broke something in me that I don't think ever fully healed.

Finally, it was time to have my son. After months of carrying him in my belly, feeling him kick, and talking to him in the quiet moments when no one else could hear me, the day had come. On January 11, 1995, my son was   born.

But it wasn't like the stories you hear about in magazines or see in movies. There was no soft music, no warm lights, no loving partner holding my hand. Instead, they had me handcuffed to a bed with officers in my room while I was giving birth. The cold metal on my wrist the uniformed strangers standing guard as I screamed through labor, reminded me that I was still a prisoner even in one of the most sacred and vulnerable moments of my life.

My doctor at that time was Dr. Hunt, a doctor out of Gainesville who helped the prison when it came to having babies and checking out all the women. He had a kind face, one of the only ones I remember from that time, and in that moment, his calmness gave me something to hold onto. I wanted to name my son Sergio Valentino after a designer I admired. Something about the name Sergio made me feel like he'd have a strong, beautiful life—like he'd be powerful like he'd be something more than what I had come from. I wanted his name to be Sergio Valentino, but the nurse convinced me that naming him Sergio wouldn't be a good idea because she felt it wasn't authentic enough for his race. I was vulnerable, emotional, and tired, and in that moment, I let her opinion matter more than my own heart. I didn't fight it. I didn't have the strength. However, I am still stuck with Valentino. And honestly, the name suits him. There's something royal about it, something unique and poetic. He was my beautiful chocolate baby with dark skin and soft, curly black hair. I remember the way he looked up at me, eyes still new to this world, his tiny body wrapped in a hospital blanket, completely unaware of the chaos he was born into.

Valentino, at that moment, was the love of my life. He was everything. He was hope wrapped in soft skin and small fingers. Holding him made everything else fade—the noise, the trauma, the walls of the prison. All I saw was him. All I felt was love. Pure, unfiltered love, the kind I had never truly experienced until that moment. I felt like maybe, just maybe, this little boy could be my redemption. My second chance. My light.

After giving birth, I was allowed to spend a few precious moments with Valentino before he was taken away. Those minutes felt like seconds. I tried to memorize every part of him—his smell, his breath, the curve of his lips. I tried to burn the memory into my soul because I knew what was coming. The separation was heartbreaking. No words can explain the ache of having your baby pulled from your arms when all you want to do is hold them forever. I knew I wouldn't be able to raise him, to be there for his first steps, his first words, or any of the milestones that mothers cherish. Instead, I had to watch him grow up from behind bars. I had to trust someone else to feed him, rock him to sleep, and wipe his tears.

And what hurt the most was knowing he would look for me one day, and I wouldn't be there. I had to trust that someone else would care for him and give him the love and stability I couldn't provide. That broke me in ways I'm still trying to heal from. Because no matter how much I wanted to be a good mother, I wasn't free. I was still trapped in the consequences of my past, still paying the price. And yet, even through the pain, I loved him. From day one. With everything I had. And that love is what carried me through the darkest days that followed.

What hurt more is that I was too scared to call Amanda to come get my baby. I was scared because I thought Amanda was upset with me. So, I relied on the State to find my son a temporary home. To be honest, I really thought I was making the best decision for myself and my son. But I had no idea that something much darker was happening behind the scenes. At Lowell Correctional Institution in 1995, the prison chaplain was involved in an illegal adoption scheme. This individual had been secretly arranging for the babies of incarcerated women to be placed with families without their mothers' full knowledge or consent. And my son was one of them. At first, I didn't realize what happened. The family that took my son seemed kind.

She lived in Orlando, Florida. She took care of me in there by sending me money when I needed it, care packages, even clothing—like jackets for the winter—and photos of my baby boy. I thought she was being generous. I was under the impression that I signed temporary custody, but it looks like I gave her my baby without knowing.

I guess not reading anything... and trusting when I should know better about trusting people. She stopped writing me, stopped sending photos, and I stopped hearing from her about my son completely. And then, one day, out of the blue, the entire compound watched as the chaplain was escorted off of the compound in handcuffs.

The truth was exposed.

I was devastated. I had trusted the system to take care of my child, and instead, he had been taken from me. I had only one person left to turn to—

Amanda. I called her from prison, barely able to get the words out. And Amanda, without hesitation, went to Orlando, found my son with the police, and brought him home. She saved him. Even after everything I put her through, even after I treated her like she was nothing, she still came through for me. She protected my child even when I couldn't. And that was when I realized just how much of a mother Amanda truly was to me. She was the only mother I had ever known.

Life in prison was harsh. The days were long and filled with a sense of hopelessness. I tried to stay strong, but the reality of my situation weighed heavily on me. I missed my son terribly and worried about his future. Would he grow up resenting me for not being there? Would he understand the choices I made and the circumstances that led to my imprisonment?

Despite the challenges, I found solace in the friendships I formed with other inmates. We shared our stories, our pain, and our hopes for the future. These connections helped me survive the darkest days and gave me a sense of belonging in a place where I felt so isolated.

As the months passed, I began to reflect on my life and the decisions that had brought me to this point. I realized that I needed to change, not just for myself but for my son. I wanted to be a better person—someone he could be proud of. I started attending therapy sessions and participating in prison programs aimed at rehabilitation. Slowly, I began to heal and find a sense of purpose.

When my sentence finally was up, I walked out of those prison gates with a renewed sense of determination. I was ready to rebuild my life and be the mother Valentino deserved. Amanda was there, waiting for me. I was going to rebuild my life over.

Reuniting with Valentino was both joyous and bittersweet. He had grown so much during my time in prison, and I felt like I had missed so much. But I was determined to make up for lost time and be the best mother I could be. I knew it wouldn't be easy, but I was ready to fight for a better future for both of us.

Looking back, I realized that my time in prison didn't teach me a lesson; it was just another chapter in my tumultuous life. I went back to prison later on, and the cycle continued. But through it all, Amanda's support never wavered. She stood by me even when I couldn't stand by myself. Her love and dedication were a beacon of hope in my darkest moments.

CHAPTER 10:
THE ROAD TO REDEMPTION

The first time, I had walked out still carrying the same anger, the same pain, the same destructive mindset that had landed me there in the first place. I thought I was free just because the door had opened, but my spirit was still shackled. I hadn't changed; I had just changed locations. The rage inside me still simmered, ready to explode at the smallest spark. The trauma still ruled my choices. I was still fighting ghosts, still blaming the world, still convinced that love was just another word for pain. I hadn't healed. I hadn't even started. I told myself I was strong because I survived, but deep down, I was tired—tired of surviving, tired of pretending I was okay, tired of carrying wounds that no one could see.

But now? Now, I had lost too much. Too much to ignore, too much to push aside. Life had stripped me bare. I had lost time, years of my life, that I could never get back. A time that should have been spent growing, laughing, and discovering who I was meant to be. Time that should have belonged to me and my son. Time that slipped through my fingers like sand, each grain a memory I would never make. I had lost pieces of myself: innocence, hope, belief in anything good. I wasn't the girl I used to be— carefree, trusting, full of big dreams. She was long gone, buried beneath the years of survival and silence. The things I had to do to stay alive, the things I endured—those things had changed me in ways I couldn't undo.

And most painfully, I had lost moments with my son—precious moments I could never recreate. His first smile, his first laugh, his first steps—all gone. I wasn't there to hold his hand when he cried. I wasn't there to tuck him in or read him bedtime stories. I wasn't there to tell him he was loved every night. And that loss? That loss haunted me. It carved itself into my soul like a permanent scar. Because a mother's love doesn't fade just because she's behind bars. If anything, it grows fiercer, more desperate, more painful. And each day that passed, I felt the weight of everything I was missing.

But I was done losing. I was done watching life pass me by. Done letting the past steal my future. I had fallen more times than I could count, but this time, I was ready to stand for real. Not just physically, but emotionally, spiritually. I was ready to fight for something better. I couldn't undo what had been done, but I could choose who I would become next. I could choose to rise. I could choose to rebuild. I could choose to stop letting my pain define me. This time, I wasn't walking out with bitterness; I was walking out with a fire. A fire to change, to grow, to become the woman my son deserved to call "Mom." And for the first time in a long time, I believed that maybe—just maybe—I could.

I had no idea what my future held, but one thing was clear: I couldn't keep living the way I had before. Something had to change.

Rebuilding from Nothing

When I walked out of those prison gates, I didn't have much. No money. No job. No real plan. But I had one thing: Amanda. She was there, waiting for me.

Just like she always had been.

Even after everything, even after I had run away, made bad decisions, and left without saying a word—she was still there. Still standing by me. Still giving me a home when she had no reason to. That kind of love? That kind of loyalty? I hadn't known what to do with it before. But now, I knew I couldn't take it for granted anymore. So, I did the only thing I could do: I went back home to Amanda's house. I was out, I was free, but freedom didn't feel like I thought it would. I was starting over from scratch, and that was terrifying.

A Woman's Prayer

By Lisa Marie Ortiz Acker

The love of my life hit me today.

I took extra care with doing my hair.

I cooked him a big meal that only he and I would share.

I cleaned the house, and I fed the kids.

I prepared the bath, and then he showed me his wrath.

I screamed and cried. I asked him why.

"Please don't do this. The kids are awake.

Please don't kick me there—my ribs may break."

Oh God, what did I do to make him treat me this way?

Should I pack the kids up, or should I stay?

God, he promised he would never do it again.

In front of his friends, I would just pretend.

Oh God, I just loved him so,

But what would become of me if I let him go?

You know what, Lord, I'll just make amends because I know in my heart
he'll never do it again.

One year later.

Remember that prayer you prayed to me that night?

I tried to reach you, but you blocked out my light.

I told you to leave, run as fast as you can.

Can't you see Lucifer has possessed this man?

Now, I'll watch over your children because that's what you need me to
do.

Heaven's gates were open, and singing with my angels, "Welcome."

Dedicated to all the women who couldn't leave but did.

CHAPTER 11:
THE STRUGGLE TO FIND MY PLACE

Even though I was free, I felt like I was still trapped. The gates had opened, and the chains had been removed, but something inside me still felt locked up. The prison had done something to me. It had changed the way I looked at the world. I didn't walk down the street the same way. I didn't sleep the same way. I didn't trust the same way. I had learned to keep my back against the wall, to watch people's hands more than their words, and to always be ready for something to go wrong. I carried that tension with me like a second skin. I wasn't the same young girl who had walked in all those years ago. That girl had been hopeful, even if it was buried under pain. She still believed in the possibility of love, of redemption, of being chosen. But the version of me that walked out was hardened, worn down by loss, and filled with a sadness that never seemed to leave.

I had spent so much time surviving that I didn't know how to just live. The concept of "normal" felt foreign. How do you enjoy a quiet day when your mind is wired for chaos? How do you plan a future when all you've ever known is instability? I didn't know how to stop looking over my shoulder. I didn't know how to rest. Every moment of calm made me anxious like peace was a setup and something bad had to be coming. I had learned how to fight, how to protect myself, how to adapt in the worst situations, but I hadn't learned how to trust, how to open up, how to just be.

I didn't know how to be a mother to Valentino. I loved him with everything in me, but love didn't come with instructions. And I was scared. Scared of messing him up. Scared of repeating the cycle. Scared that I had missed too much and that maybe he wouldn't even see me as his mom. How could I raise a child when I was still learning how to take care of myself? How could I guide him through life when I still felt so lost in mine? I was trying, but it felt like I was building a house with no tools, no blueprint, and no foundation.

How do you build a future when you've never been given a real foundation? That question haunted me. I had never seen what stability looked like. I didn't grow up with role models who modeled love or consistency. I didn't know what it meant to feel safe for more than a few moments at a time. Everything I was trying to create was based on instinct, trial and error, and hope. And sometimes, hope didn't feel like enough. But still, I woke up each day and tried because even if I didn't know the way, I knew I wanted something different. I knew I didn't want my son to carry the same burdens I had. I knew I had to try, even if I stumbled. Because trying, even in fear, was the first step toward freedom.

I didn't know how to have normal relationships or how to let people in without assuming they would hurt me. All I knew was the streets, the struggle, the fight. I wanted more for myself, but I didn't know how to get there. I tried to find a job, but who hires a convicted felon fresh out of prison? I tried to be a good mother, but how do you mother a child who barely knows you? I tried to adjust to life outside, but how do you feel free when you've never known what freedom truly is? It was overwhelming. Some days, I felt like I was drowning. Some days, I thought about running again, just disappearing, starting over somewhere new. But where would I go? I had already run from everything, and it had only brought me back to the same place.

Facing Valentino

One of the hardest parts of starting over was facing my son. Valentino had spent so much of his life without me. While I had been locked away, Amanda had been the one raising him, loving him, and giving him the stability I had never been able to provide. Would he even see me as his mother? Or was I just some stranger who had come back into his life after years of being gone? I had dreamed about being a mother, about making up for the time I had lost. But how do you step into a role that someone else has been filling? Valentino deserved the best, and I wasn't sure if I could give him that.

I was still lost. Still broken. Still trying to figure out who I was outside of survival mode. But one thing was certain: I couldn't leave him again. I had to try.

Temptation & Old Habits

Starting fresh wasn't easy. The streets were still there, calling me back. The old life, the old ways of getting money, the old cycle—it was right there, waiting for me to slip up. And I was so close to falling back into it. Because when you have nothing, and someone offers you a way to make fast money, it's hard to say no. When you feel like the world is stacked against you, it's easy to fall back into what's familiar—even if it's dangerous. And people from my past started showing up again.

The ones who only knew the old Lisa. The ones who didn't care that I was trying to change. The ones who just wanted me to go back to who I was before. And for a while, I struggled. I almost went back. But every time I thought about running back to my old ways, I thought about Valentino. I thought about Amanda, about everything she had done for me, about how she had fought to give me a second chance. And for the first time in my life, I realized I had something to lose.

Finding Strength in Myself

It wasn't easy. None of it was easy. Breaking the cycle takes work. It takes fighting against everything you've ever known. I had to learn how to stand on my own two feet. I had to learn how to love myself, even when I didn't feel worthy of love. I had to learn how to be a mother, even when I felt like I had already failed. And most of all, I had to learn how to forgive myself. Because for years, I had carried so much guilt. Guilt for running away from Amanda. Guilt for not being there for Luis. Guilt for making bad choices that landed me in prison. Guilt for missing so many moments of my son's life. That guilt could have destroyed me. But I made a choice. I chose to use that pain as fuel. I chose to fight for a different life. I didn't know what the future held, but I knew one thing: I wasn't going back.

I was going to break the cycle. Once and for all.

A New Path

By the time I had finally started finding my footing, I had no idea that life was about to throw me into the biggest challenge of all. Everything I had been through—the pain, the trauma, the survival, the heartbreak—was leading me to something bigger. Something that would test me in ways I never expected. Something that would define the rest of my life. Because everything I had been through was just the beginning. I felt like God had a different plan for me.

The real battle was still ahead.

So before I went to prison the second time, I met a man named John Smith while I was in the county jail in Ocala a while ago. After I was released from prison, we reconnected. Initially, John seemed OK, but I soon discovered he had habits that I couldn't accept—like he likes smoking crack. I don't smoke crack, so therefore that's not going to be a good match for me. Although I have been around drugs before, I've never used them, especially crack. When I moved in with John, I noticed that he wasn't treating my son well. I would come home from work and find my son in a dirty diaper. I'd find that he was hungry and hadn't been fed, and of course, that was unacceptable. So I left, and I returned to Arcadia, the only home that I knew and the only place that felt like home. I got a small trailer and started working the night shift at the Circle K, which was right around the corner from Amanda's house.

I normally walked home from work, which is what I normally do, but this particular night, the guys outside of Circle K were telling me, "Hey Lisa, like you don't need to walk home tonight. You need to either have someone take you back home or let one of us take you home. I just have a bad feeling." But of course, I didn't listen, like half the time I don't. And I received a phone call from Jonathan's mother, Patricia. That should have told me right then and there that I should have listened. But I didn't. So, while I was walking home from work—I usually took the back road, which is down the railroad tracks—I felt something behind my back. And I turned around. It was Jonathan. I'll never forget what he had on. He had on a white wife beater, a hat with a long blonde ponytail, and some jeans. And he started chasing me. He ended up overpowering me, and he raped me. And that's how I got pregnant with Marlisa.

I thought so many times to have an abortion, but I didn't because I kinda wanted a girl. And she didn't do anything to make this happen. And I'd never blamed her for nothing. She just had a messed-up father, you know. And that's how my beautiful baby girl came about. I think when she was born, just like Valentino, I was in love instantly. She was so beautiful.

But still, with my new beautiful baby girl and my son, it seemed like I just couldn't break into what I was used to. Like I wanted to do the right thing. I wanted to make a better life for my two kids. But it seemed like anything that I tried to do—I don't care if I had a job, I don't care whatever I did—it just didn't turn out right. And honestly, at that time, I picked the streets over my kids. And they will always hate me until this day because of that, especially my beautiful daughter Marlisa. To this day, she doesn't talk to me. To this day, she doesn't care if I'm alive or dead. But I caused that, not her. And I don't blame her for that either because it is my fault. If I had only made the right decisions, then things maybe would have turned a little bit different for me. So once again, as I said earlier, I chose the streets over my children. And I was back in prison again—not raising my daughter, again not raising my son, back in prison.

Like my son, she was the love of my life. But just like before, prison took me away from her, too. I didn't get to raise her as an infant. I didn't get to experience the late-night feedings, her first words, her first steps. While I was locked away, I could only dream about the moments I was missing. And the guilt? It was unbearable. By the time I got out, I had nowhere to go. But I had a friend I had met in prison: Maria.

She let me stay with her, and for the first time in what felt like forever, I got to be a mother again. Malesia's grandmother dropped her off. My son was dropped off. And just like that, for the first time ever, we were a family. I finally had both of my babies with me under one roof.

And for a moment, it felt like maybe—just maybe—life was going to be okay.

Meeting D: A Love That Turned to Pain

While staying with Maria, I met D, the man who would become my husband. At first, I thought he was the one—the man who would finally love me the way I had always dreamed of. He was a white Cuban, and once again, I experienced racism from his community for being a mixed-race woman. But I ignored it. I told myself that love could overcome anything. I believed in him. I believed in us. I believed that this was my chance at a real, stable family. And for a while, everything was good. He loved me. He was obsessed with me. He made me feel wanted in a way that I had always craved. I got pregnant with our son, Cuba. We got married. I thought I had found the life I had been searching for. But once that ring was on my finger, everything changed.

The Nightmare Begins

The man I thought loved me turned into someone else completely. He became possessive. He became controlling. And worst of all, he became violent. He was convinced that everyone wanted me. He didn't trust me, even though I had never done anything to betray him. He stalked my job, showing up unexpectedly, watching me, making sure I wasn't "up to something." The love I thought we had? It was sickening. It was twisted. It was tainted with jealousy, racism, abuse, and control. I tried to tell myself that things would get better. If I just loved him enough, if I just proved my loyalty, if I just became the perfect wife, maybe he would go back to the man he was before. But that man was gone. And I was trapped.

The Abuse

Once he put that ring on my finger, it was like he believed he owned me. He controlled everything I did. He wouldn't let me work unless he worked with me. He beat me for the smallest things: smoking a cigarette, saying the wrong thing, and not doing something exactly how he wanted.

The worst part? He degraded me in front of his family. He called my oldest son horrible racial slurs. He made me feel like I was less than nothing. He made me feel like no one would ever love me but him. And I started to believe it. I started to think that maybe this was just my fate. Maybe I was never meant to have a happy ending.

Pregnant & Trapped

Every single year we were together, I was pregnant.

First, our son Cuba. Then, our daughter Gabriella. Then, in 2005, I was pregnant again. I was exhausted. Physically. Mentally. Emotionally. I was trying to be a mother to my children while also surviving a marriage that was slowly killing me. I tried to leave him so many times. I went to a battered women's shelter, but they turned me away because of something from my past—a charge I had from when I was just a 17-year-old child.

No one wanted to help because of my past record. Not one domestic violence shelter, not one, wanted to save me. So, I kept going back. I went back over and over again. Until I just couldn't take any more.

The Final Straw

I don't know what finally broke me. Maybe it was the way he treated my children. Maybe it was the constant fear I lived in every single day. Or maybe it was the small, desperate hope inside me that whispered: You are meant for more than this.

I knew I couldn't stay. But leaving him wouldn't be easy. I was about to step into the hardest fight of my life. Because men like him? They don't let go easily. And what happened next? It would change everything.

By 2005, I was pregnant again—this time with my last child. She was my miracle baby. From the moment she was born, she faced challenges. She was born with a heart murmur and had to be airlifted for medical care. I was terrified, praying that she would be okay.

But she was a fighter—just like me. And no matter what, I loved her with everything in me. So, there I was: five kids, a husband, and a life that was suffocating me.

The Abuse My Children Witnessed

My husband's abuse never stopped. If anything, it got worse. And my children? They saw it all. My two oldest babies used to hide under the bed, trying to escape the sounds of my screams. They used to beg him to stop, their tiny voices filled with terror. They even tried to call the police more than once, desperate to protect me.

But nothing changed. I told myself, Lisa, you have to leave. But I was scared. I had no job. No money. No idea how to support five kids on my own. So, I stayed. And the cycle repeated itself, day after day, night after night.

Until one day, I finally had enough.

Leaving Him Meant Losing Everything

When I finally walked away from my husband, I thought it would be the start of something better. But it only got worse. I had no way to support all five of my kids. I had no choice but to leave some of them with their father.

I took two of my daughters—Miracle and Marlisa—and I left. To this day, that decision still haunts me. I didn't want to leave any of my children behind. I loved them all. But I knew I couldn't afford to take care of five kids by myself.

It broke me. I felt like a failure—as a mother, as a woman, as a person.

Survival Mode: Dancing, Stealing, and the streets

With two little girls to feed and no income, I desperately needed money. I turned to dancing at a strip club, trying to earn enough to keep a roof over our heads. But it wasn't enough.

So, I started stealing—just to put food on the table. And when that wasn't enough? I started selling drugs. I had promised myself I would never go down that path. But at that moment, it felt like I had no other choice.

I was stuck in an endless cycle, one that I couldn't seem to break, no matter how hard I tried.

Trusting the Wrong People

While dancing, I started using ecstasy pills, drinking a lot, and giving my body away for money. I made costumes to make extra money as well. It seems like, at that point, I lost all self-respect for myself. I got so skinny from the pills and stress; you could see my ribs. I looked horrible.

I was ashamed of myself. Embarrassed because my son Valentino knew what I was doing.

So, finally, I met an older man. He told me everything I wanted to hear—that I was beautiful, that he could help me, that I deserved more. He took me and my girls into his home. Gave us a place to stay. He nursed me back to a healthy woman so I was no longer skin and bones. I no longer was on pills, and I didn't drink anymore. He even rented a house for me in Lake City so I could be close to my children.

He was a good man. The man I'd been praying to God for.

But I didn't see that. I used him like everyone used me. And when I think about Jack… I think about the pain I caused him. How I betrayed the one good thing I had in my life.

I will always regret hurting him. At that moment, I didn't think about any of that. I just didn't care. But by that point, I didn't trust anyone. I had been used and abused too many times. I didn't know what was real and what was fake.

The only thing I knew for sure? The pain was real. And I was drowning in it.

The Spiral Continues

I was trying to survive. I was trying to be a mother. But deep inside, I was still lost. I had escaped my abusive marriage, but I had walked straight into another storm. I had no idea that the choices I was making would come back to haunt me.

I had no idea that I was about to face one of the darkest moments of my life.

Because life? It wasn't done testing me yet.

CHAPTER 12:
THE NIGHT THAT CHANGED EVERYTHING

There are moments in life that define you. Moments that scar your soul so deeply, you carry them with you forever. This was mine. This was the biggest and worst mistake of my life, one that haunts me to this day.

Dancing, Hustling, and Surviving

By this point, my life had become a blur of survival. I was dancing at the club. I was hustling, doing whatever I had to do to keep food on the table.

I was taking care of my kids while barely keeping myself together. The man I had met at the strip club—the one who had bought me a house in Lake City—had given me a temporary escape, a place to call my own. But deep down, I knew I was still trapped. I was separated from my husband, but I was still stuck in the same toxic cycle.

And then, I met G.

Another Man, Another Cycle of Abuse

G wasn't special. He wasn't different. He was just another man from the streets, living the same fast life I had been drowning in. I hated the fact that I looked for a man to give me validation or to give me love.

I felt like, at that time, that getting hit, beat on, and disrespected was love. Because that's all I knew.

At first, it was about hustling together—making money and trying to survive. I was selling dope out of the house Jack rented for us to survive. I had my girls lying in the other room. But like every other man before him, it didn't take long before he became violent. I don't know why I kept attracting these men.

I don't know what it was about me that made them turn into monsters. But every relationship ended the same way—with me being hurt. With me being abused. With me feeling like I was nothing.

Now that I'm older, I think men prey on women like me, ones with low self-esteem like myself. I had no family, just Amanda, and her family. But till this day, I've never told her. I never told her how my husband beat me or how Corey G was abusing me.

Corey G and I had been together for a few months when he started asking questions. He wanted to know about the man who had rented me the house. He wanted to know what kind of business he had, how much money he had, and what kind of connections he had. And I told him.

Then the idea came—a quick hit, a robbery, a fast way to come up. It sounded simple. We take the money, disappear, and never look back. At that point, I didn't care about anything anymore. I was broken. I was angry. I was tired of surviving. So, I agreed.

New Year's Eve, 2005: A Night I Can Never Take Back

I will never forget that night. It was New Year's Eve, the last night of 2005. The night that would change my life forever. We drove to Jacksonville, Florida, ready to put the plan into motion. The plan I made to do this was quite simple.

Maybe if my plan had been followed, we would have never gotten caught. I was supposed to be at Jack's house for New Year's Eve. Corey G was supposed to knock on the door. I answer. He hit me across the face with the gun and just robbed Jack.

But that's not how it went. He knocked on the door, but when he did, he pushed me out of the way and stated, "You're sleeping with my chick."

And it all went downhill from there. Jack started fighting back. Corey G hit him across the face with the butt of his gun until he was partially unconscious. We robbed the man who had helped me, gave me a home, fed my children, and treated me like a human being for the first time in my entire life. This is what I've done.

We forced him into the trunk of a car. And then? Before I closed the trunk, I said, "Jack, I know you don't believe in God, but you're going to die tonight. You might want to pray for your soul." And I closed the trunk with no remorse and no regret.

The person who needed to be praying was me because my soul would surely go to hell for this despicable act. I drove him into the night.

In That Moment of Pure Evil

I can still see his face. His fear. His eyes, wide with panic. His body beaten so badly by G that I didn't think he would ever be able to move again. And yet, I kept driving into the night as I listened to him struggling in that trunk, trying to get out.

And I continued to drive. As I write this, I think about that, and it still brings tears to my eyes. I can't believe I did this. Why would I do this?

Thinking back on my life, maybe I deserved what I got. Because who else but a soul of pure evil would do this horrible act?

This man had done nothing but help me. He had given me a home. He had given me money when I needed it. He had never hurt me. And yet, there I was—about to take his life.

I can't even explain what was going through my head that night. It wasn't me. It was like something else had taken over me, like I had become so numb, so angry, so broken that I didn't even recognize myself anymore.

God Intervened

That night, I drove into the forest and into the night. And when I did, something shifted inside me.

For the first time in a long time, I hesitated. Something whispered to me: "This isn't who you are, Lisa." "You weren't meant for this." "Walk away."

But G? He was waiting for me to do it. He was watching, expecting me to pull the trigger. And I had already made up my mind. If I had to do this—if I had to kill Jack, if I was the one forced to spill blood—then G wasn't walking out of those woods either. I would kill him as well. No witness, no crime.

But then, when I finally opened the trunk… he was gone. Somehow, despite his injuries, despite everything, he had escaped. I don't know how. I don't know what happened in that trunk. I still don't understand how it happened.

To this day, I ask myself: How did he escape? How did he find the strength to get out of that trunk? How did he survive after everything we had done to him?

It doesn't make sense. But the only answer I can come up with is this: God heard his prayers.

A Prayer from an Atheist

Before that night, he told me he didn't believe in God. He said he had control of his own destiny. That there was no higher power, no force beyond himself.

But when I slammed that trunk shut and told him to pray... I think he did. And I think that, for the first time in his life, he reached out to something greater than himself.

And God? He answered. Because there is no other explanation for what happened that night. That man should not have survived. That man should not have had the strength to escape. But somehow, he did.

He was saved. And in a way... so was I.

G and I left the forest terrified. We had gone there expecting to finish what we started. Instead, we left knowing that we had just made the biggest mistake of our lives.

And by the next morning, the world knew it too. Corey G swore up and down I let him go—but I did not.

The next day, the inmates that were out on the work camp found him. Half alive. They rushed him to the hospital. They put him in intensive care, barely holding on.

And then, the news broke.

The End of Life as I Knew It

The moment I saw my face plastered all over the news, I felt something inside me shatter. I knew right then and there: that was the end of my life. Not just the life I had been living—the hustling, the running, the surviving—but the life I had dreamed of having.

Every possibility, every second chance, every hope of a better future—gone.

There was no escaping this. There was no going back. I had made a choice.

And now? I had to face what came next.

A Mind Consumed by Fear and Regret

My mind wouldn't stop racing. I kept replaying that night over and over again.

The way I had stood there, staring down at him in that trunk. The words I had spoken, the threat I had made. The way my heart pounded in my chest, so full of rage and emptiness at the same time.

And then, the moment when I opened the trunk—and he was gone.

It didn't seem real.

How did he get away?

How did he find the strength to escape?

And most of all—what would he say when they found him?

I thought about how badly G had beaten him. I thought about how I had been right there, watching, letting it happen.

What if he didn't make it? What if this wasn't just a robbery gone wrong? What if this was something even worse? The weight of it all crushed me. I couldn't breathe. I couldn't think. I couldn't escape the feeling that I had destroyed everything—my life, my future, my soul. And that's when I made the only decision I could: I had to turn myself in.

The Walk Toward Consequence

The drive to the police station felt like walking toward my own execution. Every sound was louder than normal: the hum of the car engine, the sound of my breath—shaking and uneven, the weight of my heartbeat pounding in my ears. I wanted to run. I wanted to disappear. But there was nowhere left to go. Deep down, I knew I couldn't live the rest of my life looking over my shoulder, waiting for the day they came knocking on my door. I had to face it. So, I walked in.

And the moment I saw the officers, the moment they recognized me, I knew: this was it. The cuffs clicked shut around my wrists. The cold metal pressed against my skin. I was led away, step by step, toward a fate I had no control over. Everything was happening in slow motion, and yet it was happening too fast. I was no longer Lisa, the survivor. I was Lisa, the criminal. I was Lisa, the woman whose life had just come to an end.

The Death of the Old Me

They sat me down in a cold room. No windows. No warmth. No escape. And as I sat there, waiting, the reality of it all hit me like a tidal wave. This wasn't just another mistake. This wasn't just another bad decision. This was something I could never undo. I had spent my whole life fighting to survive, but this? This was the first time I had truly lost.

I wasn't just losing my freedom. I was losing the person I thought I was. And in that moment, I had to accept the hardest truth of all: the old Lisa was gone. The girl who had once dreamed of love, family, and happiness? She had died in that forest, along with whatever innocence she had left. And now? Now, all that was left was a woman waiting for judgment. Waiting to find out if there was anything left of her worth saving. Waiting to see if God still had a plan for someone like me. Because right then?

I wasn't sure I deserved one.

A Fate Sealed in Steel Bars

I knew what was coming. The questions. The trial. The sentence. I knew that soon, I would be standing in front of a judge, a jury, and the whole world, forced to answer for everything I had done. And I knew, deep down, this wouldn't be a slap on the wrist. This was real. This was forever. I had spent so much of my life trying to escape the system, but now? I had run straight into it. And this time, there was no way out.

The Beginning of a New Battle

I thought my story had ended that night in the forest. But I was wrong. Because rock bottom isn't the end. It's just the place where you decide if you're going to stay there or if you're going to fight your way out. And I had a lot of fighting left to do. Because even though I was about to face the hardest battle of my life, I wasn't done yet.

CHAPTER 13:
THE PRICE OF REDEMPTION

When I first got locked up in Duval County Jail, I sat in that cell and counted the days. I had nothing else to do but watch the walls close in and let time crawl by. 666 days. That was how long I was in the county before I was finally sentenced. Every morning, I scratched another tally on the wall in my mind, each mark a reminder of how long I had been forgotten by the system, suspended in this limbo where hope and despair blurred together. I remember looking at that number—666—and thinking, what kind of sign is this? It wasn't just a number. It was a message. It felt dark and ominous like the universe was warning me that something was about to shift and not in my favor. I had always believed in signs, little things that whispered direction or confirmation when the world got too loud. But this? This felt like a curse.

There was something chilling about sitting in that cold cell, looking at that number, knowing I was waiting on a man in a robe to decide my fate. There was no comfort, no certainty. Just silence and dread. And when the judge finally read my sentence, I knew for sure my life was over. 35 years. No parole. No second chances. The words hit me like a truck. I could barely breathe. I didn't cry. I didn't scream. I just sat there, numb, trying to process what 35 years even looked like. I was young. I hadn't even lived 35 years yet. And now, they were telling me that was how long I'd have to be locked away. That I would grow old in a cage. That the world would move on without me while I stood still behind concrete and steel.

No parole meant no light at the end of the tunnel. No milestones to work toward. No hope of early release. It meant my second chances were gone. And that crushed something in me. Because no matter how tough I was, no matter how used to loss I had become, this was different. This was final. It was a sentence not just for my body but for my soul. I felt invisible in that courtroom, like just another case number, just another name on a docket. No one cared that I was still someone's daughter, someone's mother, someone who had been through more than most people could imagine. I wanted to scream that I was more than my worst mistake. But it didn't matter. At that moment, my life didn't belong to me anymore. The system had claimed it. And all I could do was try not to disappear completely.

I was convicted of home invasion, armed robbery, and terroristic threats, and they gave me the maximum sentence. I was supposed to grow old and die in prison. And the worst part? I had been betrayed.

The Betrayal That Cost Me My Life

When I got locked up, G was still in the county, waiting for his fate. I never snitched on him. Not once. Even after everything, even after that night in the forest, I kept my mouth shut. And what did he do? He turned on me. He paid off a girl named Davida to take the stand against me. He made her lie, made her say that I did everything alone. He wanted to walk free, and he was willing to sacrifice me to do it. And for a while, it worked. The state believed them. The judge believed them. And so, I was sentenced to 35 years of my life gone in an instant, while G was supposed to go free. I was supposed to become just another forgotten soul in the system. But God wasn't done with me yet.

Fighting for My Life

When I got to prison, I still didn't know the truth. I still believed that G had stayed silent, just like I had. Until the day I found out the truth. I found out that he had betrayed me. I found out that he had lied about me. I found out that he had paid someone to set me up. And suddenly, something inside me shifted. I wasn't going to take the fall for this alone. I had already taken responsibility for what I had done. But I wasn't about to spend my life in prison while the man who planned it all got to walk free. So, I wrote the court. I begged for a sentence reduction.

And for the first time, I told the full truth. Some people might call me a snitch for that. But when it comes to my life, when it comes to loyalty, I had to open my eyes to the truth: I had been loyal to the wrong people my entire life. And I wasn't about to spend 35 years paying for someone else's freedom.

Face to Face with G

When they brought me back to Duval County for my resentencing, I saw him. Standing there in the hallway, waiting for his own fate. I looked him in the eye and asked him, "They gave me 35 years. What should I do?" And you know what he told me? "Keep that junk gangster. Do your time." Like my life meant nothing. Like I was supposed to rot away in prison while he got out to see his kids. That was all I needed to hear.

I knew then, and there I was, done protecting people who would never protect me. So, I told the truth. Yes, I did it. Yes, I was guilty. But I didn't do it alone.

A Second Chance

The court listened. They resentenced me to 15 years. I lost 20 years off my sentence. He got life. And Davida, the girl who lied about me? She got five years for perjury. She was so scared to be in the same prison as me that they had to transfer her off the compound. To this day, I still ask myself: why? Why did she lie? Why did she put herself in the middle of something she had nothing to do with?

I don't know if I'll ever understand it. But what do I know? God gave me another chance. And I wasn't about to waste it.

Surviving 15 Years in Hell

Prison was not easy. It was hell. I've seen people die in there. I've seen women get trapped by officers and have babies in there. I've seen officers kill inmates, then blame it on inmates and beat them without reason. I was one of those women. I remember one time exactly— I let Roberson woke me up with a can of black Jesus in my face and then opened the door to beat me. All for something I said a few days before. Captain Graff—he was known for hurting the women in there. He also went into my cell and sprayed me in my face with black Jesus and left me in a cell with no clothes or food for days. Black Jesus is a very strong pepper spray that's made for bears. But they use it on the women in prison if they don't obey.

I've been trapped in there because of my looks, confronted by the female officers like I was just an average woman. Free, they would be upset because their boyfriends or husbands would work at that prison, and they would try to proposition me for sex. I had access to drugs, cigarettes, makeup, and anything any one of those inmates wanted because of the way I looked, how I carried myself, how I was no-nonsense all the time, and how most of the time I kept my mouth shut unless I had to tell—and that was mostly if my life was in danger.

It was a time when I was at F.W.R.C., which stands for Florida Women's Correctional Institution. And I wasn't spared from any of it. Never was. My 15 years was hard. Officers took advantage of their power. I was used and abused by the same people who were supposed to "protect" me. I got shanked. I got beaten. I got thrown into a system that was designed to break me. And yet, I survived. Because I knew, deep down, that God still had something for me. I wasn't meant to die in that prison. There was a reason I was still here. And on January 2, 2021, I finally found out what it was.

Freedom, At Last

After 15 years, the gates finally opened. I walked out of the Florida Women's Correctional Institution as a free woman. And as I stepped outside, I felt something I hadn't felt in decades: hope.

I had spent years blaming God for everything that had happened to me. But now? I realized that it was God who had carried me through it all. He could have let me die in that prison. He could have let me stay lost. But He didn't. He brought me back. And I knew, standing there outside those prison gates, that my story wasn't over yet.

The Ones I Lost

But freedom came with a price. Of all my children, only Valentino ever wrote me. Only he ever came to see me. My ex-husband hated me so much that he made sure I never saw my babies. I wrote them every single birthday. I wrote them every single month. But I never heard back. And Marliese? She was taken by the state. She was put into foster care, and now? She won't even speak to me. It breaks me.

But I know that if God could give me back my freedom, He can give me back my children, too. And I will never stop praying for that.

I Will Never Go Back

Prison took 15 years of my life. But it didn't take me. And when I walked out those gates, the last thing I heard was the voice of Captain Copeland, one of the officers. She said, "Inmate Fundora. I'll see you again." I turned to her, and in my heart, I knew: No, you won't. Because I will never go back. Not to prison. Not to that life. Not to the person I used to be. Because God saved me for a reason. And I intend to find out what that reason is.

Bouncing from Place to Place

With nowhere to live, I went to stay with a girl I had met in prison. But the moment I walked into her house, I realized something: she was still living the same life that got her locked up. I had spent 15 years in hell, and I refused to walk back into it. I didn't go through everything I went through just to end up right back where I started. So, I left. I called another girl from prison, one who lived in St. Petersburg, Florida.

She welcomed me in. She didn't have much, but she let me stay on her couch with her and her kids. She didn't have to do that. But she did. And I was grateful.

The Hustle Begins Again, But This Time, It's Different

I didn't have a car. I didn't have money saved up. But what did I have? Determination. I walked to work every single day—10 miles there, 10 miles back. I saved every dollar I could. I didn't go out. I didn't waste money. I focused on one goal: getting my own place. And after a few months of grinding, I did it. I got my own apartment.

No furniture. No decorations. Just four walls and a roof over my head—and to me, it was the most beautiful thing in the world. Because it was mine. I kept saving. I bought furniture piece by piece. I bought a car. I found a good job that paid well. For the first time in my entire life, I felt like I had some control over my future.

And just when I thought things were finally falling into place, something happened.

Something I never saw coming. Something that, for a moment, felt like a miracle.

A Message from My Oldest Daughter

My oldest daughter, Marlisa, reached out to me.

After years of silence, years of not knowing if she would ever want me in her life again, she found me. And she had a question. She wanted me to do the Ancestry DNA test. She wanted to find out where we came from. So, I did it. And what I found? Something I had been searching for since I was a little girl. I found my mother. I found the family I had lost.

I found the answers I had spent my entire life chasing. But instead of feeling joy, instead of feeling relief, I felt heartbreak.

My mother looked just as I imagined—dark, beautiful skin and long hair. She was so beautiful. And she was my mother: Leslie Woodruff. I spoke to my mother for the first time in my life. I spoke to my siblings— the ones I never knew I had. I found out that after she gave me and Luis up to the system, she had four more kids. She had a whole life.

And we? We were never a part of it. I bought plane tickets for her to come see me. I bought plane tickets for my sister. Twice.

They never came. Not once. I tried. And I tried. And then, my mother finally told me the truth: she didn't want to meet me. She said I was crazy. She said none of her kids turned out like me or Luis. She said I would never have anything, never be anything, never amount to anything.

And for the first time in a long time? I felt like that abandoned little girl all over again.

I had spent my whole life waiting for this moment. Waiting for my mother to come back for me. Waiting for her to tell me why she left. Waiting for her to love me the way a mother is supposed to love her child.

But that moment? It never came.

Letting Go of the Dream

It hurt. It still hurts.

Imagine spending your entire life waiting to meet your family, trying to find out who you are and where you came from—and getting rejected like you did something wrong.

I still don't understand why she wouldn't want to meet her daughter. Why wouldn't she want to ask me those questions, like: Lisa, how was your life? What's your favorite color? What do you like to do?

But she treated me like it was my fault. At three years old, I had a decision to leave her. I will never understand this. And I will never understand why she's rejecting me.

Does it hurt? Yes, it does. But what can I do about it?

But now? Now, I see things clearly.

I wasn't the problem. She was.

She had four more children. She had the chance to come looking for us. She had the chance to save us from the hell we went through. But she chose not to. And that's not on me. That's on her.

I wanted a mother who would love me. I wanted a family to call my own. But now I realize God had a different plan for me.

My Testimony Is My Strength

There was a time when I blamed God for everything that happened to me. I blamed Him for taking my childhood. I blamed Him for taking my freedom. I blamed Him for making me suffer for so long.

But now? Now I know that every battle I've fought has led me here to this moment.

Because my testimony isn't just mine.

It's for someone else who needs to hear it.

Someone who has been used and abused.

Someone who has been beaten down and left for dead.

Someone who has been abandoned, rejected, told they were nothing.

And to that person?

I am living proof that they can survive.

I am standing tall, with two feet on the ground, saying:

"Yes, you tried to destroy me."

"You tried everything to break me."

"But look at me now. I survived."

Without God, I would not be alive.

Without God, I would not have the life I have now.

Without God, I would not be able to tell my story and help others tell theirs.

I am not my past.

I am not my trauma.

I am not my mother's rejection.

I am who God says I am.

And this? This is just the beginning.

The End... or the Beginning of a New Chapter?

Some stories end in tragedy. Mine? Mine is just getting started. Because after everything I've been through, I finally understand my purpose.

And the best part? I'm still here to live it. My name is Lisa Ortiz Acker, and this is my story.

Final Thoughts:

Luis has been in prison for 25 years. My brother, my best friend, the one who always ran with me, survived with me, endured with me. He's still behind bars, paying for the life we were born into, the cycle we couldn't escape. And I carry that with me every single day. But I know one thing: his story isn't over either. Just like mine wasn't.

A New Purpose, A New Legacy

I am no longer the girl running from her past. I am no longer the woman trapped by her mistakes. I am a survivor. I am a fighter. And today? I am a businesswoman, a designer, and the owner of my own clothing line—something I never thought would be possible. I have taken the pain, the struggles, the lessons, and I've turned them into something greater.

Giving Back: The Mission That Drives Me

I dedicate my life now to helping those who are still trapped—the men and women still behind bars. The lost souls who think their past defines them. The broken hearts who believe they will never be whole again.

I do prison outreach, speaking to those who feel forgotten, hopeless, and abandoned. I remind them that God is real. I remind them that their mistakes don't define them.

I remind them that they, too, can be redeemed.

Keep Pushing Forward

If you're reading this, and you feel like your life is over, like you have no way out, like you've made too many mistakes to ever be forgiven—I am proof that you are wrong.

God has a plan for you. God can turn your pain into purpose. No matter where you are today, no matter what you've done—keep pushing forward. Because the day will come when you look back at your life, and instead of seeing all the pain, all the regret, all the things that tried to destroy you—you will see a testimony. You will see a survivor. You will see the person God always intended you to be.

And that? That is worth fighting for.

The End. Or Maybe, Just the Beginning.

This is your final chapter, but it's not the end of your story. Because every single day you wake up, you are writing a new one. And I have no doubt that God is still working on the next chapter of your life—one filled with purpose, redemption, and the blessings you never saw coming.

Because you are not your past. You are proof that miracles exist.

GOD IS REAL.

This book is dedicated

to

Amenda Walker

ABOUT THE AUTHOR

Lisa Ortiz, based in Florida, is a survivor, mentor, and the voice behind She Wore Her Scars Like Wings. Her life in the system, marked by abuse, trauma, and resilience, led her to write this raw and powerful memoir.

She is the founder of JustAckerDesigns, a bold and inspiring clothing line created for everyday people with a love for wild, expressive fashion on a real-life budget. Beyond fashion, Lisa dedicates her life to prison outreach and mentoring abused women and girls, using her past pain and hard-won lessons to guide others toward healing and hope. Every step of her journey is grounded in faith, and she gives all glory to the One above.

"JustAckerDesigns"

My brand is called "JustAckerDesigns". I make everything from custom clothing to 2-piece original sets and dresses. We also make customized items as well. I make clothing for the average person who just wants to be their self.

YOU CAN CONTACT ME
THROUGH MY SOCIAL MEDIA PAGE:

 **: justackerdesigns**

 **: justacker_designs**

 **: Accer Des**